THE PROP BUILDER'S
MOLDING & CASTING
HANDBOOK

THE PROP BUILDER'S
MOLDING & CASTING
HANDBOOK

THURSTON JAMES

BETTERWAY BOOKS

BETTERWAY BOOKS
CINCINNATI, OHIO

Cover design by David Wagner
Typography by Typecasting

Every precaution has been taken in preparing *The Prop Builder's
Molding & Casting Handbook* to make these projects as safe and successful as possible. However, neither Betterway Books nor the author
assume any responsibility for any damages or injuries incurred in connection with the use of this manual.

Other fine Betterway Books are available from your local bookstore or
direct from the publisher.

07   06   05   04   03   15   14   13   12   11

Library of Congress Cataloging-in-Publication Data

James, Thurston.
    The prop builder's molding & casting handbook / Thurston James.
        p.   cm.
    Includes index.
    ISBN 1-55870-133-8—ISBN 1-55870-128-1 (pbk.)
    1. Plaster craft. 2. Molding (Founding)—Amateurs' manuals. 3.
Plastics—Molding—Amateurs' manuals. 4. Stage props—Design and
construction. I. Title. II. Title: Prop builder's molding and casting handbook.
  TT295.J36   1989
   792'.025—dc20
                                                                89-36138

Acknowledgments

I am under some obligation to Marsha Frank–Burke, editor and author, for her work in editing this series of books on property construction techniques. She helped me to find an order to a very wide ranging subject. As the texts received their first exposure to editing, Marsha unknowingly taught me a subject I refused to take seriously in high school: how to communicate in written English. I am grateful.

I want to thank Rob Secrest, a molding and casting expert from the Albuquerque area. He read a first draft of this text and made many helpful comments. Rob was also available for regular consultation as the final text was being completed.

I am indebted to Nick Bryson, President of Gerriets International, for developing the basic design of the vacuum forming machines which are demonstrated in the final chapter of this book. I appreciate the work done by Jeff Wachtel, Principal Electronic Technician for The Department of Theater at UCLA, as we modified this concept to build a vacuum forming machine specifically for use in producing properties.

LaVahn Hoh of the University of Virginia read, reviewed, and criticized the final manuscript. His careful reading and concerned comments prompted the rewriting of several sections.

I acknowledge The Department of Theater, Film, and Television at UCLA for allowing me to use the theater facilities during my off-duty hours to photograph the properties for our productions as they were being made.

CONTENTS

MAKING THE CASTINGS (Continued)

VACUUM FORMING WITH THERMOPLASTICS 175

APPENDIX 223

PREFACE

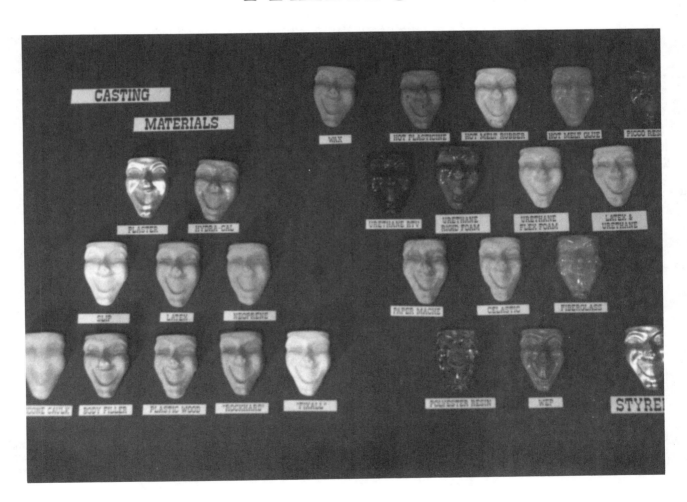

The Materials of Molding and Casting

This book will demonstrate the methods and techniques for using thirty different molding and casting materials, ranging from papier-mâché to breakaway glass. No assumption has been made that the reader has any previous experience.

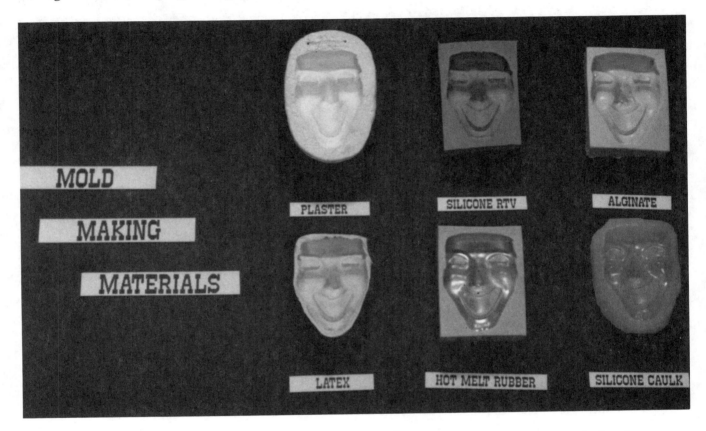

The mold-making materials include plaster, two kinds of alginate, two forms of silicone rubber, latex, and hot-melt rubber.

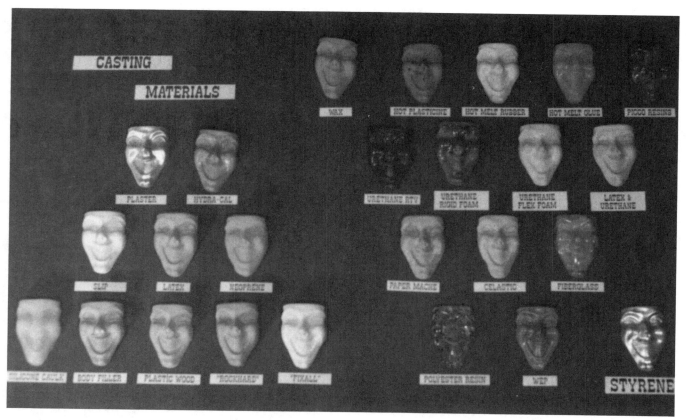

Casting materials long familiar to theater technicians—plaster and its cousins and Celastic—are covered with the same thoroughness as the more recent flexible plastics which have been developed: latex and three variations of polyurethane.

Thermosets are discussed with an emphasis on the polyester resins, fiberglass, and water extendable polyester.

A series of materials which become liquid when heated to their melting point is thoroughly demonstrated. The "hot melt" materials include wax, hot-melt rubbers, and hot-melt picco resins used in the manufacture of breakaway glass.

The section on slipcasting shows how a newer product, neoprene, uses an age-old pottery process to great advantage in the theater.

Products found at local hardware stores in the form of putties and caulking compounds are included, showing their unique features and how they can be pressed into service as casting materials when nothing else is readily available.

Near the end of the book is a section devoted to the construction of a vacuum forming machine. The instructions are intended to aid an experienced electrician and metal worker in the special problems encountered in building this large tool. This is the only portion of text that is not directed to an inexperienced person. The final chapter explains some techniques of using this machine or any of the commercially made vacuum forming machines being found in increasing numbrs in university and community theater scene shops.

How to Get Started

How does a person go about learning the techniques of casting and mold-making? Here are some of the ways:

1. Attend workshops
2. Apprentice with an "old timer"
3. Jump in, experience trial and error, and learn by doing
4. Read product literature and experience new materials as they come along
5. Read a book

Begin with any of these and work your way through them all. Maybe all of the ways will not be open to you. That's probably O.K. — do what you can. These are all good ways, and they all have their limitations. Let's touch on each of these methods, and discuss some of their advantages and disadvantages.

Workshops

In most cities, hobby shops and plastic suppliers conduct workshops as a means of showcasing their products. If your supplier does not have this service, you might at least arrange for the demonstration of certain specific products you are interested in. The problem with even a well-organized workshop is that there is limited time provided in which to demonstrate a time-consuming subject. In three or four hours you can only be introduced to three or four products, and these only in the most basic fashion. But at least you will have been introduced.

Apprentice with a Working Craftsman

This is a good idea if you have the time and really are serious about learning the craft. Search out a mold maker with some experience, spend some time with him, and pick his brain. Count yourself as very fortunate if you can place yourself with a mold-making craftsman. Keep your mind open, realizing that even experts have prejudices and favorite methods, and very frequently they do not agree with other experts.

I do not believe that mold-making and casting experts are an endangered species. They have just become more specialized. You will find them in the porcelain and ceramics field, in aerospace, as tool and pattern makers, in plastic toys, plastic packaging, and plastic products of all kinds. The motion picture audiences' thirst for the bizarre has produced a market for a wide variety of aliens and extraterrestrials. Most of the designers of these monsters are not old timers, they are comparative youngsters. And speaking of youngsters...I was recently in the curators' workroom at the Museum of Natural History in Los Angeles, where the staff was working with junior high schoolers making latex impressions of delicate tropical ferns for use on the museum's wild animal exhibits. The museum was getting a large volume of authentic-looking plastic foliage, and the kids were getting a hands-on experience in the technique of mold-making.

Jump In and Try

Experience is a great teacher. After you have picked up a little knowledge of a material, use it. Make sure you understand its hazards and how to use it safely; then pile in. If you have had little or no previous experience I suggest you begin with plaster, latex rubber, and neoprene. These are relatively safe materials to work with, they are inexpensive, and the chance of success is high. As you gain confidence with these materials, branch out into other materials, building on the knowledge you have acquired with these first experiments. Always keep alert to the toxic potential of the product you are about to use and guard against its danger. You will soon become your own expert. It won't be long before you can pick up literature on a newly introduced plastic product and use it more comfortably than the chemist who developed it.

Read a Book

Not a bad idea. Don't overlook this resource. There are some very good books on the market. Most of them are specialized. You will find books devoted to the subjects of plaster casting, polyester, moulage, and several on fiberglass casting.

The book you hold in your hands provides a broad-based introduction to the craft. Reading has its limitations too; it's got to be backed up by *doing* for the learning to take place. Have fun getting smart.

A Word About Failure

If your personality is one that cannot run the risk of failure, you may be in for some psychological trauma. Frequently, your early work will be failures. If you are working with someone who has had previous experience with the materials, perhaps he can tell you why. Don't look to your mentor expecting godlike qualities — he will have failures too. Usually the "old timer" will know enough to use an untried system or process in private until he is comfortable with it. Then he can show it off without spoiling his reputation as an expert. Well, good for him! That technique is, in itself, one that is acquired as the result of experience.

You must expect occasional unusual results.

They happen. If the shelf life of some products is exceeded, they may not give the expected results. If some plastic chemicals become contaminated, they will not work as expected. If you work for a long time with resins, the time will surely come when you forget to use a mold release, or you will use the wrong catalyst, or you will forget again and use no catalyst at all. These mistakes will bring predictably unsuccessful results. You will be able to understand immediately why your casting failed as soon as you realize your mistake. But there will also be the times that you will run into freakish, unreasonable problems that defy explanation.

SAFETY

Protecting Yourself from the Effects of Hazardous Chemicals

The Surgeon General has determined that smoking cigarettes is hazardous to your health. Many people have quit—some of the public is stubborn, however, or suspicious of authority, or naïve, or gullible, because this element of the public continues to smoke with all confidence. ''We have been doing it for a lifetime without serious consequences, and therefore, the Surgeon General must have his facts confused.''

Thirty-five years ago, craftsmen began receiving similar warnings concerning the chemicals in the plastic materials they work with. Warnings concerning the toxic effects of some of the new polyester and epoxy resins, solvents, lacquers, aerosol sprays, and dyes. The attitude of the artists and craftsmen to whom these warnings were directed was, at first, very much like the attitude of the smoking public: ''I know what I am doing, I have been doing it for a long time without any problems, and these threats are being published by a bunch of alarmists.'' The term *chronic long term effects* was not widely known then, and those who did know, chose not to deal with it.

Becoming Aware of Health Hazards

Some of the products which have ''been around for years,'' such as asbestos, were actually proven to be doing fatal damage to the lungs. Cancer became linked to specific carcinogenic chemicals such as benzine. Skin rashes broke out as a direct result of some of the other solvents that were being used. Slowly, an awareness dawned upon these craftspeople that the warnings were perhaps more than just threats. **Too often, however, the attitude continues that the danger is for those others, and not myself.**

Do You Need an Attitude Adjustment?

What do you think? Are these labels put here by the manufacturer with a serious concern that you might be injured with improper use of the product? Or do you, the consumer, look suspiciously at these clear warnings as disclaimers that the manufacturer must make for his own protection on the rare chance that someone might be injured?

Who should be most concerned about potential risks to *your* health? Society at large? Government agencies? Manufacturers of useful chemical products? You yourself? Who can you trust to be most responsive to your health needs? Without removing the responsibility from others, I propose that you **selfishly become accountable for yourself.** Take the steps necessary to make yourself aware of the dangers of chemical products. If you are unaware of the dangers of the chemicals of molding and casting, or if you are guilty of using these chemicals without proper safeguards, please read the next few paragraphs with a self-concerned, open mind. I will outline some of the dangers of the chemicals used in molding and casting and propose ways of using them safely. **You, the user, must then take the necessary precautions to protect yourself from their ill effects, which can, at their worst, be life threatening.**

The Toxic Assault on Our Bodies

Toxic substances can enter your body in three ways: by contact with skin, by inhalation, or by ingestion through the mouth. We are familiar with the dangers of taking poisons through the mouth. We have known since childhood that arsenic, cyanide, strychnine, and hemlock are likely to kill if they are eaten in any quantity, so we are careful not to do that. We have learned that babies will get sick if they eat paint, bleach, or gasoline, so we don't do that either—or do we? We have habits that cause harm to our bodies that we are unaware of. I have known people to pick dried Celastic from their fingers with their teeth. Some artists have been taught to put a point on their paint brushes by taking them into their mouths. The practice of having a filled coffee cup at the work table where it is sure to become contaminated is common. The published warnings on chemical packages warn us to wash our hands and refrain from smoking. Part of this warning has to do with fire dangers, but the other part is to reduce the possibility of transferring these poisons to our mouths and thus swallowing them.

The most frequent way that toxins are introduced into the body is through the nose. Dusts, fumes, gases, and vapors can cause direct damage to the respiratory system just as smoking can, except that the dangers from chemicals can be greater. All solvents and aerosol cans admonish the user to use the product in well-ventilated places. Why don't more people do it? Maybe we don't know that when they say "well-ventilated," they really mean "use in a spray booth," or "use by an exhaust fan." Inhaled toxic gases can also be absorbed into the bloodstream. In exactly the same way that the life-supporting gas, oxygen, is absorbed and transported, poisonous vapors are absorbed and distributed where they can do their dirty work on their favorite body organ. This organ usually turns out to be your liver, heart, lungs, kidneys, or brain.

Finally, poisons can get to your organs through your skin. Cuts, abrasions, and open sores that allow blood to leak out of the body will also allow chemical poisons to get in. Some solvents, however, do not even need this kind of doorway to get into your living space. They can work their way into your bloodstream through the pores of your skin. Other chemicals—battery acid, lye, and gasoline—attack the skin itself, causing burns or rashes. There are also many less offensive but nonetheless noxious chemicals, some of which you will encounter while working with the materials explained in this book.

Degree of Risk

Industrial hygienists have recently been devoting time to studying the dangers that plastics workers are exposed to. They have worked out some definitions useful in explaining these dangers. They say that there are three factors which contribute to your "degree of risk" in working with chemicals.

First, there is the amount of exposure to a single toxic substance. There are three things which contribute to this exposure. They are:

1. The quantity of the material you are exposed to
2. The duration of the exposure
3. The frequency of the exposure

The cumulative effect of all the separate exposures to chemicals is called your "body burden." When your body burden exceeds your capacity to eliminate the encountered poisons, injury to some part of your body takes place.

Another factor that must be considered in figuring your degree of risk is that some chemicals are much more dangerous to the body when combined than when either one is encountered alone. A good example of this complication is the case of smokers who are exposed to asbestos fibers. Smokers have about ten times the chance of getting lung cancer as non-smokers; however, the risk is multiplied again by nearly ten times when these smokers are exposed to asbestos fibers. Their risk of getting lung cancer is ninety-two times greater than people who are exposed to neither.

The last factor you should consider in figuring your danger or risk in working with toxic materials is **your own susceptibility or sensitivity to chemical injury.** Some people are more sensitive to the harmful effects of chemicals than others. A problem with this is that people who are not sensitive have the idea that they are immune to the dangers. This is a mistake! It just means that your body's protective systems are not yet overloaded. Keep it up, and you can overtax your body's abilities to protect you. Injuries will certainly result.

You probably already know by experimentation whether you are skin sensitive to the exposure of harsh chemicals. It is not as easy to detect your sensitivity to liver or kidney damage or to cancer. And it is not wise to experiment till you know the limit.

Now, all of this has been said to instill a respect for the problem, not to frighten you unduly into a resolve to never again come in contact with another chemical. You could drive yourself crazy trying to eliminate this contact. In this world we live in today, we are constantly in contact with potentially dangerous materials. But you can become aware of the more dangerous products, and choose not to use them. You can use the less hazardous consumer products, and use them with precautions, thus greatly reducing your body burden.

You can read and heed the warnings published on the cans of chemical products. Most warnings can be summarized in the following list:

1. Use solvents and sprays in well-ventilated places, and away from flames.
2. When working around dusts, mists, sprays, and vapors use properly fitted respiratory protection.
3. Use non-porous gloves or barrier creams.
4. Wash your hands well after working, especially before eating.
5. Wear overclothing (a lab coat or apron) to avoid taking toxic dusts home to your living and eating spaces.

This list contains good advice, but obeying the can warning is only a beginning.

If you are really interested in becoming responsible for your own health and well-being, you can take some, or all, of the following precautions.

1. Request Material Safety Data Sheets from the manufacturers of products you have any questions about.
2. Do some reading. Research the chemicals in the products you are using, and learn how they are evaluated for relative toxicity. See the bibliography at the end of this book.
3. If you choose to use a material which is advertised as potentially hazardous, provide all of the engineering controls you can. Install spray booths and/or exhaust fans. Make sure you have and use personal protection: safety glasses, respirators, gloves, and aprons.

Personal Protection Equipment

Let's take just a moment, and talk about some of the equipment that can protect your eyes, lungs, and skin.

Glasses and Goggles

Eye protection is available in the form of safety glasses or goggles. Eyeglasses are usually clear, non-prescription, and primarily designed for protection from dust and sparks. Some safety glasses come equipped with side shields which make them more effective against these flying particles. Goggles, however, provide the best defense against chemical spills.

Gloves

Many kinds of gloves are available, each is useful for protection against a particular harmful material.

A very inexpensive glove made of polyethylene is sold in paint stores to protect the painter from getting his hands soiled. These gloves are not good for much except painting. The chemicals of molding and casting very soon dissolve these thin attempts at protection.

Thin latex gloves are recommended for most molding and casting operations that could chemically affect your skin. These gloves are usually green (like surgeons wear), are very thin, and do not totally eliminate your sense of touch.

Thick leather gloves with high cuffs that completely cover the wrist are good protection against hot liquids. Care must be taken not to allow hot liquids to pour into the large, blousey cuffs. Leather gloves are available as standard equipment from welding suppliers.

Neoprene gloves are impervious to almost all harsh liquids, even acids, but are thick and clumsy, and not necessary for protection against any of the chemicals mentioned in this book.

Respirators

Breathing protection is of two distinct types, and if you are to operate safely you must understand the distinction. A respirator has a changeable cartridge and can be used in defense against both types of respiratory hazard.

The first type is protection against particles. A surgical mask is helpful in filtering mist and dust particles. A dust mask is better, and a respirator fitted with a particle filter is also quite good.

The other type is protection against vapors or fumes. It is essentially a gas mask. For a respirator to control the intake of fumes, it must be fitted with a fume cartridge.

If a respirator is going to be effective against anything, it must fit your face well and be strapped securely to your head. A respirator is ineffective when worn over a beard. The craftsman who works constantly with polyesters or urethanes must sacrifice his facial hair.

In Conclusion

Once you are well-informed, you can make rational decisions about whether you consider a product dangerous, and whether you have the facilities to use it safely. Frequently you can substitute a safer product for a product you decide to be too hazardous.

When you select a material for a particular job, always look on the selection as being tentative — check to see whether you have the knowl-edge and special safety equipment (exhaust fans, fume hoods, safety glasses, respirators, gloves, aprons, and confidence) the process requires. If you cannot perform the necessary steps safely, choose another material!

You see, you really are not being forced to use potentially hazardous materials. If, however, you choose to use them, choose also to use them safely.

THE MODEL

Molding and casting is a process involving three distinct stages:
1. Selection and preparation of the Model (or pattern)
2. Making the mold
3. Making and finishing the castings

Preparing the Model

The first step in mold making is the consideration of the pattern or model. In the following pages you will be led through the steps of making a vase, a fish, and a milk pitcher. Each of these will be copied from a real, "found" model. On the other hand, you might want to make a thing that isn't readily available, or perhaps that no one has ever seen before. You might need Aladdin's magic lamp, or a space gun, or Excalibur, or Cinderella's glass slipper. If you want a fantasy item, you must sculpt your own original.

Sculpting a Model

If you must design and sculpt the model from your imagination, wet clay and non-drying clays (commonly known as "Plasticine"—trade name held by Peter Pan Playthings Ltd.) are good modeling materials. Non-drying modeling clay is available in a wax base or oil base and in four grades of softness or workability. No. 1 is very soft. This clay is useful on large projects where you need to push around large masses of clay. It moves easily, but sometimes it moves so easily that it won't hold its shape.

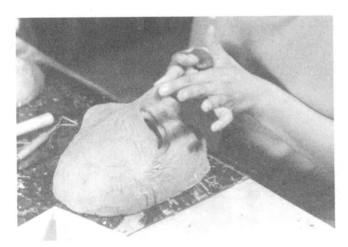

No. 2 and No. 3 are utility grades of modeling clay. They work well where you want to work fast and the features you are trying to produce are not extremely fine.

No. 4 is the firmest. It works best with clay working tools. The smallest details will hold their shape while the mold is being made.

As you gain experience with the materials of mold making, you will find that some materials are not chemically compatible with others. For instance, the sulphur content in oil-based clay will inhibit the curing of silicone RTV rubbers. Therefore, you must not make a model of this oil-based clay if you plan to make the mold in silicone. I mention this because it is one of the considerations of model sculpting that must be dealt with.

If you are inexperienced, you should begin by sculpting your model from either wet clay or oil clay, and making your mold in plaster.

Keep the model simple enough that you can get away with a one- or two-piece mold. If you design your model with undercuts that appear in both the front and side views, the pattern cannot separate from the mold, and you will be in for some troubles. If you use a found object as a model, you may find it necessary to alter the original, filling in undercuts with modeling clay, and definitely patching over holes that pass completely through it.

The more complex shapes can certainly be accomplished with multiple part molds, but they are not easy and in my experience they are rarely necessary. You will be well advised, as you start out, to make some simple compromises in the figure you sculpt or select, so that it can be accommodated by a two-part mold.

Defining Some Terms

The words *mold* and *cast* have become somewhat intermixed by common usage. But the dictionary assures me that *mold* has a preferred meaning which is: "A form that gives a particular shape to anything in a fluid or plastic condition." *Cast* has a preferred meaning which is: "The shape which is formed in a mold." I will attempt to use these words in their preferred definitions. In the following pages you will be directed to make a casting of a pattern which will then become a mold for making additional castings. This can only lead to some confusion, but perhaps now that you are aware of the verbal problem, we can still communicate. I will use the words *pattern*, *subject*, *model*, and *object* to describe the original form (sculpture or authentic item) which is to be reproduced.

Efficiency

You may, on occasion, find yourself casting an item when it is clearly not the most efficient thing to do. If you only need one or two copies of an article, weigh the time and trouble of mold making and casting against the possibility of sculpting all of the items you need directly from urethane foam or papier-mâché. Sometimes you will be ahead to use the original sculpture and skip the mold-making process entirely.

THE MOLD

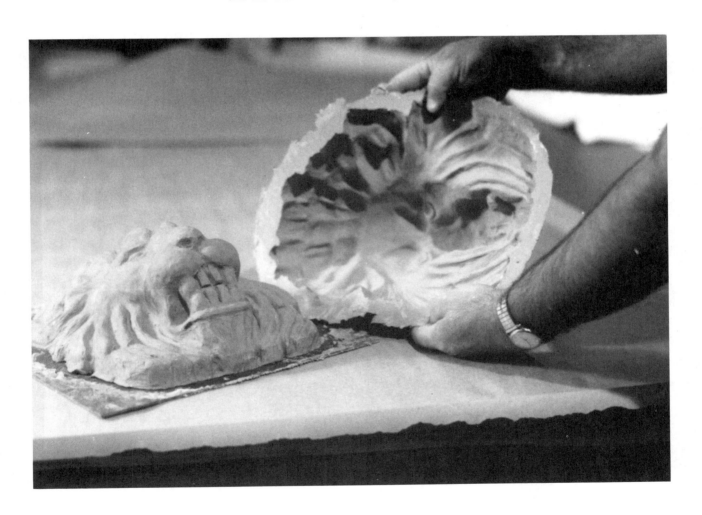

Undercuts—The Need for Multiple Part Molds

An undercut is an indentation in a side facet of a pattern (or mold) that allows a casting material to get a locking grip on its surface. Undercuts prevent easy removal of the casting and are usually avoided at all costs. On the rare occasion that you feel an undercut is necessary, you must take steps to accommodate it: plan from the beginning to construct a flexible mold (silicone); or if you choose to work from a hard material (plaster), deal with the problem by making a multiple-part mold.

A One-Part Mold

Frequently a model can be reproduced with a one-part mold. The patterns shown here are illustrative of the simplest kind of pattern; one that lies flat on a table or against a wall, so its backside is completely concealed. All the lines taper away from the perimeter of the pattern and toward the center of the piece.

No undercuts are produced. The designer of such an item usually feels no compromise when he is denied the option of a negative draft in the side of his sculpture.

A Two-Part Mold

Most of the ceramic and porcelain items you have in your home (vases, figurines, dishes, bottles) have been designed to be cast from a two-part mold.

These figures have been made from a two-part mold. An examination of any one of them will show the seam line which the casting has retained as a minor flaw where the mold halves joined together. You could trace the seam line of the central figure (the discus thrower) up the left leg to the knee where it joins the right arm, around his head, and along the top of his left arm, around the discus, back along the arm, down his left side, and down the column that supports the figure to the base.

Although the figure seems complex, there are no undercuts. All of the lines radiating from the seam line taper ever so slightly to the center of the figure.

Multiple Part Molds

Sometimes a figure is structured with undercuts that can only be obtained from a plaster mold made of many parts or a flexible mold.

The wings on both of these figures contain deep undercuts that were deliberately carved into the sculpture. If you wanted to make reproductions of this pattern the undercuts would have to be dealt with.

Flexible silicone molds have replaced multiple part plaster molds in almost every instance. The absorption casting process is an exception to this rule. (More on this later.)

Mold-Making Considerations

The construction and preparation of the mold is the most important single step in the process of turning your model into a series of cast reproductions. You might spend hours designing, sculpting, and perfecting your model, but if the mold is not well made and well thought out, and if you do not spend enough effort on the selection and application of mold release, your beautifully designed pattern can become waste. Effort in this early stage of the process will be more than paid for as you begin cranking out clean, flawless castings from a perfected mold.

There are several different materials that can be used to make good quality molds. You will find that these materials have a wide variety of characteristics. Some are solid, some are more flexible; some are cheap, some are more expensive; some have good reproductive qualities, and some are truly excellent.

"Hard" and "Soft" Molds

Plaster is the most common of the hard molding materials. Plaster molds can be made and used when your model and the castings you intend to make are soft (flexible). Soft models would include objects like a face, a foot, an apple, a fish, or anything made of clay. Soft casting materials include all of the various members of the rubber family: latex, neoprene, the silicones, and some of the urethanes. Polyester resins and fiberglass are considered "hard" and will only separate from a plaster mold if the casting is pulled before it is fully cured, and therefore slightly flexible. If you wait for it to cure and harden, you might have a terrible time pulling the casting from the mold.

Reproducing Fine Details

The reproductive qualities of the various molding materials vary greatly. You are probably familiar with the fidelity in which plaster works; if you are making an impression of a hand, you can, if you work with care, take away a copy of the subject's fingerprints. You may not know, however, that the law enforcement agencies have found that by using another casting material, silicone rubber, they can make a cast impression of even the latent fingerprints which have been left on a handrail.

Alginate molding materials are used for making prosthetics (reproductions of parts of the human body) and anywhere you want good reproductive results. Alginate is, however, a very temporary material. It dries out quickly and shrinks badly.

CASTING PLASTER

Casting plaster is made of gypsum or calcium sulfate. The manufacturer bakes all of the water out of it with a heat so extreme, even the water which has been molecularly bound in the compound is released. The residue is then ground into a fine powder.

When you reintroduce water to the powdered gypsum it forms a complex of tightly interlaced crystals. As these crystals take shape, they solidify into a kind of cement. Each manufacturer makes several grades of plaster which vary in their setting times and in their strength and hardness. It would seem that in this day of high technology, some plastic product would have been developed to replace this old standby as a mold-making material, but nothing has. For the price, the ease of working, the relative safety, nothing beats plaster for most utility molding and casting.

Types of Plaster

Our shop uses two kinds of plaster—industrial casting plaster (Plaster of Paris) and #1 Pottery Plaster; and one mortar material—Hydra-Cal. All are trade names of products made by United States Gypsum Company.

Casting plaster or plaster of Paris works easily and will set up in about twenty minutes. It is inexpensive and is easily available at lumber yards in 100 pound bags. Plaster of Paris is packaged in five pound boxes and is available from art stores and hobby shops, but three of these five pound boxes can cost the same as the lumber yard 100 pound bag, and it is essentially the same powder in them both. You can use casting plaster satisfactorily on any job that calls for a plaster mold. It can be used with success on absorption castings or as a hard form for making many copies of other casting materials.

No. 1 Pottery Plaster is formulated to be extra absorbent, and is therefore to be preferred on all operations where you are going to use the slip casting procedure.

Hydra-Cal isn't really a plaster, but more a kind of cement or mortar, much like dental stone. It sets up much harder than casting plaster, and will withstand repeated use. Because of its strength it also stands a better chance of retaining intricate detail that could break or chip if the casting were made in plaster.

No. 1 Pottery Plaster and Hydra-Cal are not nearly as readily available as casting plaster. You will probably have to get these products from a dealer who handles supplies for ceramics and pottery workers.

A Two-Part Plaster Mold

Many of the objects that you want to cast will require a two-part mold, the two pieces of the mold separating down the middle. The joint will make a seamline, and it's up to you to locate this seam in such a way that it will minimize undercuts and be as inconspicuous as possible.

Molds are sometimes made by submerging a pattern into wet plaster, but this procedure nearly always traps air bubbles under the object. In the following discussion, you will be directed to make the first half of the mold by pouring plaster over the form, then, after turning the unit over, pouring plaster to make the second half. Proceeding in this manner, you will always be pouring plaster onto the top of the form. Air bubbles are less likely to form when you use this technique. They are still possible, but you are lengthening the odds.

A vase and a fish will be used as patterns in the following projects. The vase is a typical sort of object that you might want to cast. The fish is rather atypical. The techniques of casting, however, are largely the same.

All undercuts that will not slide easily from the mold must be eliminated. If you find an undercut such as the one in the bottom of the vase, fill the depression with Plasticine. The opening of the vase must also be plugged. Neither the fish nor the vase have any other serious undercuts, but if there were any they would have to be searched out and filled.

Build a box to surround the object that you are going to cast. It will contain the wet plaster till it solidifies. The box should be at least one inch bigger in every direction than the size of the model being cast. Construct this box with double headed nails so it can be easily disassembled.

Build a shell of Plasticine around your pattern till exactly one-half of the object is covered. This clay shell will surround the bottom portion of your pattern, protecting it from the plaster when it is poured. The exposed part will make up the first half of your plaster mold. A seamline will be formed at the precise placement of this clay shell. With "hard" patterns (such as this vase), it is critical to locate this seamline on the midline of the object. If you can find the original mold line on bottles, it is an excellent guide for making this mid-line.

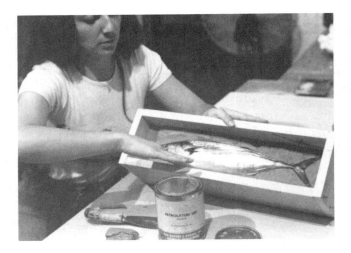 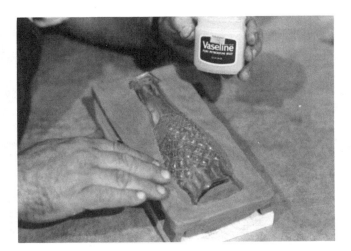

Apply a releasing agent to the model being cast and to all of the wooden surfaces of the box. Petroleum jelly is a good release agent to use when you are working with plaster. A very thin coat is all you need. Avoid filling fine details in your pattern with a heavy coating of this release

agent. Do not, however, skip any areas; everything must receive a thin coating. Plaster will not adhere to the fish or to the oil based clay, but coating these areas will do no harm, and will only assist in separating the casting from the pattern.

Safety Considerations

Casting plaster is a comparatively safe material to work around. The dust is slightly caustic and a respiratory irritant. It contains talc and silica which can be very fine and not clear well from your lungs, but the dust is heavy and does not fill the atmosphere, so breathing it should not be a problem when you are working with it in small quantities. Skin contact with plaster, in either powder or liquid form, is somewhat dehydrating, so the use of a little petroleum jelly or hand lotion on your hands will help prevent skin dryness.

High heat can be generated as plaster cures. Do not attempt to copy body parts with plaster.

This is not an idle warning! There are cases on record where fingers have been lost, burned beyond recovery, because they were imprisoned in the cast and could not be released from plaster as it began to cure. The safe material to use for prosthetics is alginate, which will be explained in a subsequent section (see pages 43 to 48).

1. **Wear dust mask when working with large quantities of plaster.**

2. **Use petroleum jelly or hand lotion before and after skin contact with plaster.**

3. **Never attempt to cast body parts with plaster.**

Mixing Plaster

Plaster manufacturers recommend that plaster and water be mixed by weight. The recommended ratio for plaster of Paris is about five pounds of water to eight pounds of dry plaster. Making a solution that has too much (or too little) water in it will greatly reduce the plaster's strength. The method of mixing shown here will bypass the weighing process, but the proportions of water and plaster are still approximately correct.

Estimate the volume of water that you will

need — about two-thirds the volume of the air space in the box. When the proper amount of plaster is added to the water, the volume will increase by the remaining one-third. (Hydra-Cal uses less water than plaster, so your estimate of water should be considerably less with this product — maybe as much as twenty percent less.) Tap water should work fine. Colder water will slow the setting time; hot water will speed it up. Always sift the plaster into the water, and not the reverse.

Sift the plaster into the water without stirring. Keep adding plaster until the entire surface of the bucket is covered with a moist mud-like coating. Wait several minutes. If this plaster "landfill" should soak up too much plaster and sink, you must add more powder till all of the liquid is soaked up and the surface is covered with damp plaster.

It must be emphasized that this method works only if there is no stirring of the mixture till this muddy landfill is formed. Do not get impatient. Allow the plaster another five minutes or so to soak in the water.

Now stir. Stir the mixture thoroughly without whipping it. Violent stirring will pick up air and mix it into the plaster. Air bubbles left trapped in the plaster show up on the finished casting as pits and holes. This kind of failure is preventable, and many of the techniques of working plaster are concerned with eliminating air bubbles. The mixture should be pourable — about the consistency of thick pancake batter (not *thin* pancake batter, mind you, but *thick* pancake batter).

Pouring the Plaster

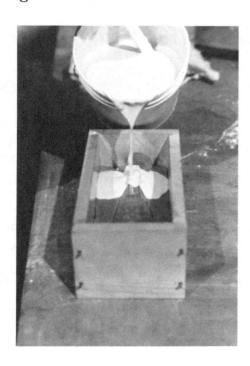

The plaster should be used immediately after mixing.

To eliminate churning and the formation of air bubbles, pour the mix into the lowest corner of the box. As you continue pouring, the plaster level rises, gently flowing around the pattern, making close contact with all parts of its surface.

Tap the box gently on all sides with a hammer. Repeated tapping shakes the pattern, loosening any air trapped in the mixture, and bringing it to the surface of the wet plaster.

Plaster sets as the result of a chemical process and is not a matter of drying. The chemical reaction causes a good deal of heat. The heat is not normally a reason for concern, but it is something to be aware of. It is best to wait overnight before continuing. This allows the plaster to harden, cure, and gain some strength.

However, in the case of the fish, there is some reason for hurrying. We don't want to allow Mr. Fish time to decompose. The heat given off as the plaster does its chemical thing has already taken all the chill off the fish. Since you must rush the process, only wait long enough for the plaster to harden and cool off, and then continue carefully, so that the soft, fragile plaster is not damaged.

Disassemble the box. Be careful not to dislodge the pattern from the mold. You are not yet ready to admire the results of your work.

Turn the casting over and remove all of the Plasticine. (If you are careful not to get a lot of plaster chips trapped into the Plasticine, it can be set aside and stored for future use.)

Keying Notches

Using a coin or a large washer as a chisel, scrape two or three holes ½″ deep into the surface of the soft plaster. In the next step, as this two-part mold is completed, these scooped depressions will appear on the face of the second half of the mold as pronounced bumps.

When the mold's halves are mated, the bumps snuggle into the depressions. These keying devices assure perfect alignment.

Reassemble the box around the inverted casting.

Grease the whole form, the pattern, the box, and the plaster surface of the first half of the mold with a thin coat of petroleum jelly.

Pouring the Second Half

Mix the plaster as before, and pour it into the box. Don't forget to tap the box to remove air bubbles. Wait overnight for the plaster to cure.

In the casting of the fish, however, there is reason for rushing the process to prevent cooking the fish.

Remove the box, separate the cast halves, and remove the patterns. If you intend to make a lot of copies of an object, it might be a very good idea to make two complete molds so you can make the reproductions twice as fast.

We were even able to make two castings of the fish before it began to decompose.

Drying Plaster Molds

As was noted earlier, plaster casting is a chemical process and not a matter of drying. This is true, but you should know that plaster crystals have a great quantity of unused water trapped in them. You'll notice that as the molds dry for a week or two, they will lose a good deal of their weight as this excess water evaporates. A drying period of a day or two is helpful if you plan to use the molds in an absorption casting system. Latex, neoprene, or slipcasting require all of the absorption qualities that only a dry plaster mold can provide. Note: It is possible for a mold to become *too* dry. More of this in the section on absorption casting (pages 85 to 98).

If you are going to use the molds with a catalyzed casting material, they should be allowed to dry before you seal them and apply any mold release.

It is a good idea to dry large molds for a couple of days with the two halves strapped together. Molds can warp during cure-out, and clamping helps keep them registered to each other.

A One-Part Plaster Mold

A simple pattern, one designed to have a side lie flat against a wall or table or somehow be hidden from view, and one that has no undercuts in its shape, can be reproduced by casting it in a mold made of just one part. The casket handle mounts illustrated in this project are ideal for demonstrating the one-part mold.

This hardware was taken from one of the least expensive "John Doe" type caskets. The finished coffin can be seen in the section on Neoprene Casting Rubber (pages 96 to 98). The steps in constructing the plaster mold, however, are demonstrated here.

A one-piece mold could make use of a wooden box similar to the one illustrated in the previous section. However, another method of controlling the flow of the liquid plaster will be demonstrated. The mold makers adept at this technique claim that it is faster and easier once you get the hang of it.

Always begin any plaster casting process by preparing the pattern, searching for undesirable undercuts, and filling in all holes. This pattern has no objectionable undercuts, but there is a hole in each piece designed to receive the handle. The hole is necessary and will be cut into the casting as it is made in a later step, but for now this hole must be filled with Plasticine in order to make the plaster mold. Shape the clay plug in such a way that a clear outline is retained in the casting so this hole can be cut with precision.

The larger piece shown in the photo is designed to fit on one of the corners of the casket. The 90° corner which is built into the hardware is preserved in the casting by mounting it on a triangular slice from a 4 x 4 wooden post.

Mix up a batch of plaster, like the "pancake batter" mentioned before.

When no box is used, the plaster is controlled

It should take three or four minutes to finish the impression coating. Go immediately on to the next step.

Build a low wall of modeling clay about ¾" from the base of the model and completely surrounding it. the use of this barricade is recommended to ensure the plaster casting has a uniform thickness at the base, which is neither too fragile nor wastefully wide.

Cover the entire form with a light coating of a mold release. Since we plan to make the castings in neoprene rubber, liquid soap must be used as the release agent. (See the section on Neoprene Casting Rubber, pages 96 to 98, for further explanation of this requirement.)

by manipulating the mixture, timing its use as it gets progressively thicker and thicker and finally hardens.

Make an impression coating with the thinnest part of the plaster mix. Use your fingers to spread this covering. There is no easy way to escape using your hands as you control the flow of the plaster.

Continuously tap the surface of the pattern with your plaster wetted finger guaranteeing that there is unbroken contact between the pattern and the impression coating. No air pockets can be allowed to form between this coating and the surfaces of the mold.

Scoop up a handful of plaster and squeeze it gently from your hand to the impression coating. Work patiently. Repeat the operation again and again till the pattern is covered as well as possible, and the retaining wall is filled to the point of overflowing. Control the flow and keep it on your pattern and off your table. As the plaster thickens, continue piling it slowly and patiently, till the pattern is coated with a covering at least ½" thick in all places.

When the mound of plaster is the consistency of butter, work on it with a putty knife.

Rub the surface of the mold with your hands and a little water to smooth its exterior. Some mold makers are as concerned with the appearance of the outside of their molds as they are with their interior perfection.

After the plaster gets firm, warms, cools, and then has had a chance to cure for a few hours, the pattern can be removed. This photo shows the pattern and the finished plaster mold which was taken from it. A mold such as this should be allowed to set for several days to dry out before it is used.

A Two-Part Mold — Shim Method

An alternative technique of making a two-part mold involves the use of a clay sculpture and small pieces of thin gauge sheet metal. The clay pattern must be soft to allow the thin metal strips to saw their way a short distance into its interior, dividing the pattern in half and locating the seam.

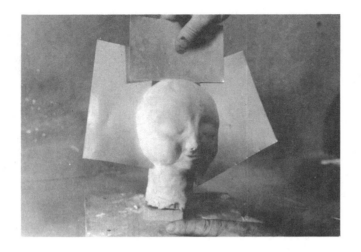

Decide where you want to place the seam line, and mark it by making a light tracing around this circumference. Use this line to guide you as the shims are slipped into the soft clay.

Be careful that you don't shove the shims into the model too deeply, cutting the pattern in half. Use a pair of tin snips to cut a slight arc in the shim so it doesn't penetrate too far into the pattern. Or use several smaller shims. When you use more shims, each shim only has to slide in a short distance.

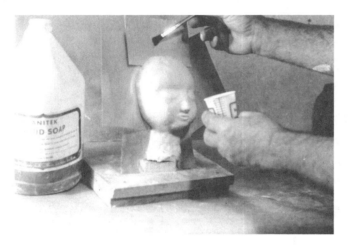

Coat the shim material with a release agent. We have a choice here of using either petroleum jelly or liquid soap — let's use soap. The clay will not adhere to plaster, but a little soap applied to the clay surface can only help.

Lay the pattern in a cradle (made of a large coffee can or an empty paint bucket) so the weight of the unit is resting on the shims very near where they enter the clay. The shims must be supported

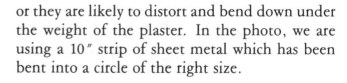

or they are likely to distort and bend down under the weight of the plaster. In the photo, we are using a 10″ strip of sheet metal which has been bent into a circle of the right size.

When the pattern is resting comfortably, mix up a batch of plaster as explained on the previous pages and apply the necessary impression coating to eliminate air bubbles.

Pile the plaster onto the form slowly and patiently until it is covered to a thickness of at least

½". As it gets thicker, work the surface with a putty knife and smooth the exterior of the mold.

When the plaster has solidified and cooled, you can begin to handle it. Remove the shims.

The rim bordering the pattern should be flat and smooth. If there are slight stairsteps in the surface of this rim where the shims overlapped,

scrape them smooth with a knife blade.

Dig out a few keying holes to aid in accurate mating, and the first half of the mold is about finished.

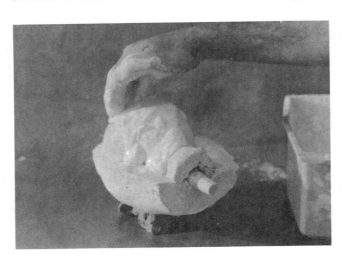

Soap or grease the plaster that has been exposed by the removal of the shims, so the second pouring will not stick to it. Pour the second half following the same steps used before: make an impression coat, and then build up a mound of plaster. Smooth the fresh plaster to conform to the rim made by the first pouring. Let the mold set up overnight to attain maximum strength.

Gently tap around the seam of the mold with a knife blade and a hammer to jar the halves loose. Separate the mold halves, and remove the pattern.

Clean up imperfections in the edges where the molds join, mate them, bind them with a restraint, and the mold is ready for use.

This mold could be used with the materials of slip-casting, either with latex, neoprene, or with low fire slip clay.

It could be used as a form to build shells of papier-mâché, Celastic, Plastic Wood, or polyester resin and fiberglass.

Or it could be used to cast copies of latex and flexible urethane foam. You can see a completed

copy of this doll head made of urethane foam in the section on Hair Implanting (page 156).

ALGINATE

Alginate, manufactured from a kind of seaweed, is the only really safe material for the casting of human body parts. The dentist who makes perfectly fitting dentures is the big user of alginate. You may have experienced this product yourself, flavored strawberry, mint, or wild cherry, while sitting in a dentist's chair. It is flexible, very fast setting, will not adhere to anything (not even itself), and has excellent reproductive qualities.

One regrettable feature of this process: if the pattern is at all complex, you will only be able to make one casting from an alginate mold. Alginate is soft and fragile, and there is no way of successfully removing the casting with deep undercuts, except by cutting away the mold.

Alginate comes as a dry powder and is water mixed. The finished mold remains very moist.

Prosthetics

Prosthetics is a medical term referring to the branch of surgery that deals with the molding, casting, and fitting of artificial body parts. The term has expanded in its usage to include the activities of the makeup artist who casts body parts for the purpose of making perfectly fitting noses, chins, or masks, and the magician who casts lifelike limbs for use in dismemberment illusions.

Dental Alginate

To demonstrate the techniques of working with alginate, we will make a negative mold of a hand, and then make a positive reproduction cast from plaster.

Before you begin mixing the alginate, discuss with your model the hand shape that you are hoping to achieve. Once the hand is in the alginate, neither of you will be able to see the pose of the hand and your subject will be guided only by the memory of what that position felt like. Don't ask for an excessive curve on the fingers. Keep the hand position simple or it may be impossible for your model to remove his or her fingers from the casting without destroying it.

Measure your subject's hand, and make a box about an inch bigger in all directions than these measurements. Alginate is very thin and will run away, sliding off the hand and onto your work table without a box like this to control the fluid before it sets up.

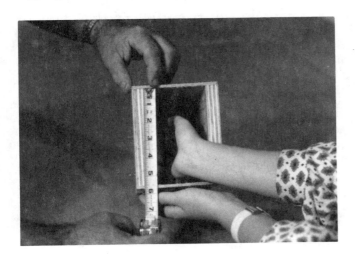

The alginate is packed with a measuring scoop and a small vial, handy for attaining the correct proportions of powder and water in the making of one dental impression. You will probably need about fifty scoops of alginate (depending on the size of your box) and about fifty vials of water.

Pour the liquid into a large mixing bowl and then add the powder to it. Immediately begin to stir the mixture with a wide blade spatula (such as is used for mixing a cake) or with an electric mixer. In fact, the mixture should look a lot like cake batter. The mixture should be somewhat pasty, but pourable. When you become familiar with this product you will be able to judge its viscosity and add more water or powder as needed till you get the right feel. You must not hesitate in making this decision, however, because "normal set" dental alginate is very fast acting and will solidify in just three minutes. That allows about forty-five seconds for you to mix the alginate, fifteen seconds to pour it into the box, and two minutes to adjust the hand's position in the paste.

The set time can be slowed to about ten minutes if you use ice water in the mixing. Warm water will speed up the set time, but who could want less time than three minutes? Teledyne makes a prosthetic alginate that is specifically for makeup and special effects and is designed to set up in about fifteen minutes. So you have several choices.

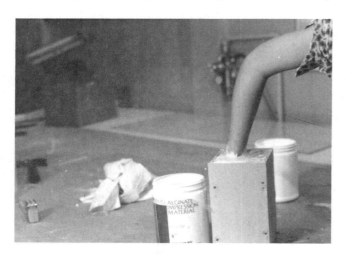

Pour the alginate in the box and have your model insert his/her hand into the thickish mixture.

The proper distribution of the alginate around the hand and fingers must be done by the "cast-ee," whose hand is in the box. This step must be done by the sense of touch, and you as the "cast-or" are deprived of the necessary information to be very helpful. Your model will know, by feeling, where the thin places are, whether they are at the knuckle or the fingertips, and can push the paste around to do something about it.

Your subject will know when the paste begins to gel and must then stop all hand movement. He or she should hold the hand immobile in a natural position and wait the few minutes it takes for the alginate to set up.

After the alginate sets up, remove the nails and disassemble the box.

Have your model begin to very gently flex his fingers to break the seal that exists between the hand and the mold. Work patiently from the wrist down to the fingertips. Lift the mold slightly at the wrist and the subject will begin to feel this separation occurring.

The moist alginate is flexible enough that (with a little luck) your model will be able to withdraw his hand through the uncut wrist hole. If it looks like this will be impossible, you can make one cut in the mold, along the thumb, to allow for the withdrawal of the hand. The slit in the mold can be made with the dullest of table knives, because the alginate is so soft. Still, the model will probably appreciate it if you let him do the cutting. He will be able to feel the blade making contact with the skin and will know how deep to scrape. If your subject has a slender hand, this slit can be very short or perhaps not necessary at all.

If your model has been working patiently and consistently, wriggling his fingers loose, he should be able to announce to you that his hand is free from the tight confinement of the gelled alginate, and the hand can be withdrawn from the mold.

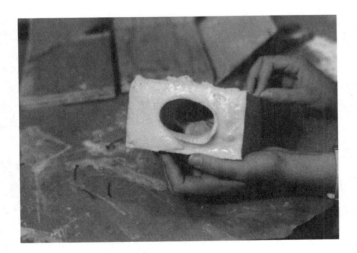

The model's hand will come out of the mold cleanly. The only flaw in the mold would be in the place where you made a slit along the thumb, if indeed that was necessary. You will be reasonably certain of having a seamless mold if you use a prosthetic grade alginate instead of the kind dentists use. It is more flexible and tear resistant, so your model's hand can be withdrawn without slitting or doing any other damage to the mold.

The mold remains moist and should not be used with any casting process whose curing would be inhibited in the presence of water. Plaster is completely compatible with alginate and is recommended for use in this mold.

Prepare a mixture of plaster, and pour it directly into your mold. Pour each finger separately, and with care. Stop pouring when the fingers and thumb are full of the casting material, and bounce the mold on the table to dislodge any existing air entrapment. Do this quickly, and then finish filling the palm and wrist of the mold.

Set this aside for an eight- to ten-hour period. The plaster should have plenty of time to set up and cure.

Do not be impatient to see the finished product. If you attempt to open the casting prematurely, you run a great risk of breaking off the fragile fingers.

After the plaster has cured (at least overnight) begin to cut away the alginate mold.

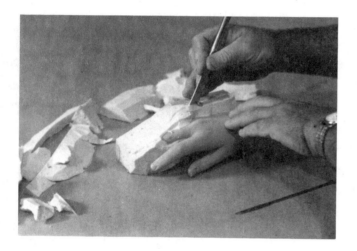

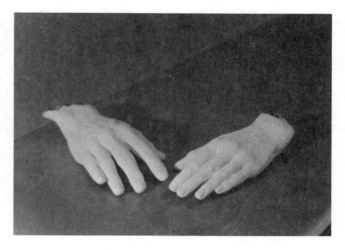

Alginate is capable of duplicating very fine details, so you can expect every wart, mole, wrinkle, lifeline, heartline, scar, and fingerprint to be faithfully reproduced.

These finished hands have been painted with an air-brush to give them a natural, lifelike coloring.

Distortions and Shrinkage

Distortions are an inherent problem with alginate. But there are ways of taking care of them. Very often, a plaster support, called a *mother mold,* must be made to keep the flexible alginate in its intended shape. (See the section on Mother Molds, pages 58 to 60, for a complete explanation of this process.) The mold of the hand we just made doesn't have this problem, because it has sufficient cross section to make it strong.

It is a curious fact that an alginate mold will shrink a lot as the moisture evaporates from it. Shrinkage is not a big problem for our purposes if we use the mold within a day or so, but a dentist is cautioned to make his casting within the hour, or it will not fit his patient's mouth. Even during this short wait time, the dentist will keep his alginate mold wrapped in wet cloths.

If you want to save an alginate mold for a maximum amount of time (maybe as long as a week), wrap the mold in wet cloth, put it in a Ziploc food bag, and keep it in a refrigerator. Do not, however, attempt to save the alginate mold while it is still nested in the mother mold. The plaster mother mold would suck a great deal of moisture from the alginate as it cures out. This is the very thing you want to avoid.

It is interesting (and might even be useful) to see the kinds of distortions that can be made by pouring plaster into an unsupported alginate mold. In the following pictures, the mother mold had been removed, and the weight of the plaster was allowed to spread the mold.

This is a comparison of the castings of a supported and an unsupported mold of a life mask. When the mother mold is removed the nose broadens and the face fattens and flattens.

Here we have a graphic demonstration of how an alginate mold will shrink as it dries out. From right to left, we have a casting from the supported mold, from the unsupported mold, from the unsupported mold three days later, and from the unsupported mold one week later.

Moulage

Moulage is another alginate material made from kelp. In the 1930s and 1940s, moulage was widely used in medical circles for taking impressions of diseased internal organs (livers, kidneys, and the like). These castings were made for comparative studies and instructional purposes. Law enforcement agencies of this same period were also big users of moulage in preserving the evidence of footprints, tire tracks, etc.

Moulage is different from the other alginates just described in several ways.

1. It is a globby seaweed gelatine even in its bulk form. You will find it shredded and moist when you take it from the package.
2. Moulage is a hot melt. When you heat it to about 150°F. it becomes fluid and formable.
3. A big advantage to the constant user of moulage is that it is completely recyclable. Simply reheat it, adding moisture occasionally as it dries out, to make it fluid and reusable.

The following series of photos illustrates how moulage can be used to reproduce decorative wood molding from a bureau drawer.

We prepared the pattern by surrounding it with Plasticine to control the moulage while it is liquid.

Moulage is a better molding material than plaster for this job because it is flexible. A hard plaster mold would most likely break—either when you attempted to remove the original pattern, or when you tried to release the copies (also made from a hard material).

Take a couple of handfuls of moulage from its airtight package and drop it into a pot. If the gelatine is not moist and properly jelly-like you might have to add a small amount of water. Heat the moulage in a double boiler till it begins to melt and flow. The melting point is low — about 150°F. — so it will become liquid in a very short time.

Use a wide-blade spatula to mix the heated liquid moulage. You will find the wide blade useful in squashing the solids against the side of the pan and in breaking up lumps. Soon the combined effect of the heat and stirring will produce a creamy paste.

Use a spatula to ladle a wad of the creamy moulage directly onto your model. Work the mixture slowly onto the pattern till it is entirely covered, without any air bubbles, to a depth of ¼".

In a very few minutes the moulage will be cool. The mold is flexible. In fact, it is so flexible that it needs to be reinforced with a plaster mother mold.

Mix up a batch of casting plaster and lay it directly onto the still-damp moulage to a depth of about ½" to make a supporting mother mold.

For best results, this mold should be used almost immediately. Moulage has the same drying and shrinking characteristics that all alginates possess.

The reproductions must be poured with some casting material that is compatible with the moisture that is remaining in the moulage. Any of the water mix materials of the plaster or mortar family will work fine. I chose to use a polyester product. See the section on Water Extendable Polyester (pages 145 and 146) for instructions on how to make castings from this mold.

RUBBER MOLDS

Latex Rubber

Liquid latex rubber is a formulation of milky juices from certain rubber trees, with preservatives, solvent (ammonia), and other ingredients; but it is mostly those milky juices.

You can use latex rubber for making flexible molds, or for making cast reproductions from other mold materials. In either case the cured latex becomes a strong pliant skin of formed rubber. Latex curing comes about as ammonia solvent evaporates from the liquid rubber.

Safety Considerations

This product is one of the safer materials to use. The ammonia is not concentrated and when liquid latex is used in small quantities there is little hazard. Breathing a heavy concentration of ammonia vapors, however, can irritate your lungs and cause fluid to form there. Heavy concentrations of ammonia vapors can also cause eye damage.

SUMMARY: Use latex in a space that has good general air movement.

Latex Mold

A latex mold can be made by coating an object with liquid latex rubber. When the rubber cures, a skin is produced, so flexible that it can be peeled off a simple pattern in one piece leaving no seam line. It peels off over itself, like a surgeon removes his glove, but when this latex glove is turned right side out it is ready to be used as a mold for making reproductions.

Examine and prepare the object that you will be using for the molding pattern. Ideally, the pattern should have a slight taper from its base to its top. Slight undercuts will present no problem. Hourglass shapes and reverse tapers should be avoided — the rubbery skin could be stressed beyond its stretch limit as you remove it and it might tear.

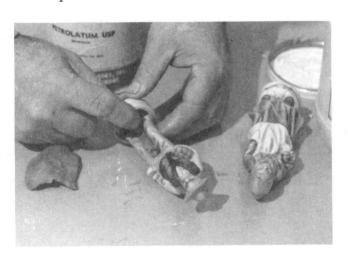

Holes that pass entirely through the figure must be filled with Plasticine. Otherwise, the glove-peeling analogy would become a topological impossibility. (A pair of trousers cannot be removed intact by pulling them over your head, whereas a dress is removed easily in this manner.)

Latex may tend to stick to the figurine. To keep the latex from sticking to the pattern, coat the clean, dry pattern with liquid soap or aerosol silicone mold release. If you use an oil or grease, the first coat of latex will tend to slide down the figurine into a puddle at its feet. (It is also important to know that an oil-based release agent will deteriorate rubber.)

After the release agent (soap or spray mold release) has dried, dip the prepared figure into liquid latex.

Set the pattern aside to dry overnight. The drying time on an object this small can be reduced by force drying the latex in a low heat oven. Just remember what you are trying to do. You want to drive the ammonia out of the liquid rubber, not cook it. Any drying technique that you are familiar with, such as air movements or external heat, could be used to accelerate the drying time. A hair dryer is very effective at force drying latex rubber. Forced drying will definitely increase the amount of ammonia vapors released into the air and should only be done when good ventilation is employed.

When the latex coating is dry to the touch, it is ready to be dipped a second time. The latex sticks better this time, filling all voids that might have been missed in the first dipping. Sometimes a third and a fourth coating will be necessary. It all depends on the viscosity of the latex formulation you are using.

The formulation used in the photos is thick enough that two dippings make a satisfactory mold. Another coating would make the mold less flexible. While it would hold its true shape a little better, it would also be more difficult to peel the mold over itself.

After the mold has cured (dried out), it can be removed from the pattern.

Lubricate the outer surface of the mold with a little liquid soap to make the surface slippery.

Peel the rubber skin off the pattern. The soapy lubricant allows the rubber to slide over itself easily, with a minimum of stress. Grasping the mold with a firm grip and pushing the figurine on the top of the head with a thumb is a good system for removing the pattern.

Casting a Figure from a Latex Mold

While the mold is wrong side out, rub a very light coating of soap over the interior of the mold, which is now exposed and easy to reach. Turn the mold back on itself again so the mold is right side out. The latex shell is now waiting to be used as a mold for making reproductions.

Calculating the Volume of Your Mold

When the product you are using for your casting is expensive, it is helpful to know just how much material is needed to fill your mold without waste. Here is a simple way to calculate the volume of the mold. (The product used here is not especially expensive, but let's take a look at the process while we're here).

First, you fill the mold with water. This is the amount of liquid it will take to fill the mold... but how much is it?

Pour the water into a measuring cup to know the answer. To fill our mold, about a cupful of casting material will be needed.

This is extremely elementary, but perhaps it is one of those things that is not readily apparent until it has been pointed out.

After the plaster has set up and gained some strength, the exterior of the rubber mold should again be soaped up in preparation for its removal.

Fill the mold with a casting material. We are using plaster in the illustration.

If you were casting a large object, it is likely that you would have to reinforce the mold with a plaster mother mold. On a small mold of this kind, however, the latex rubber has enough strength to withstand the weight of the poured plaster and not distort.

Remove the mold by sliding and peeling it inside out. If you grasp the base of the figure and attempt to *pull* the casting out of its cocoon, the casting will most likely break off at some thin or narrow area (probably the neck), so don't do that. Instead, grab the skirt of the skin of the mold and *push* the figure through the mold with your thumb or a push stick.

Latex is susceptible to deterioration from minute chemical particles suspended in the atmosphere. Armorall, made by the McKesson Corp., Irvine, CA, is a very good preservative for latex molds (or castings) when you want them to last for prolonged periods. It also seals latex and will protect it to a certain extent from the degrading effects of any petroleum products it might come in contact with.

Silicone RTV Rubber Molds

Silicone RTV (room temperature vulcanizing) rubber is usually your best choice, when you are searching for a mold-making material. It has all of the good characteristics that you would want in a mold-making material!

Silicone rubber can reproduce details so fine you cannot detect them with your naked eye. Silicone molds are used in medical applications in which researchers preserve, copy, and study *cell layers* of diseased organs. This is pretty exotic stuff, far exceeding the needs of mold making for theater applications. You may think that it is extravagant to use an expensive material which can achieve reproductive detail too fine to be detected by the naked eye—and if that were all there was to it, you would be right. But there are other desirable qualities of silicone that should be considered. Let's just say the reproductive properties are good, and go on.

Silicone rubber requires no mold release. The silicone mold will peel right off—with ease. You can cast any material in a silicone mold and it will separate without any prying, chipping, or cursing—and that is worth a lot.

Silicone rubber is flexible. You can make molds of irregular shapes containing undercuts. There are limits to how far your mold will stretch and how much undercut you will be able to reproduce (you would have trouble reproducing a winged cupid in a one-piece mold); but if you stay within the bounds of reason, I feel secure in saying that silicone molds can be used to reproduce undercuts.

Silicone rubber is tough. The mold is resilient. When you stretch it to release from an undercut it rebounds to its original shape. It is also highly tear resistant. These good stretch and rebound characteristics hold true even in thin sections. A silicone rubber mold will last a long time even with repeated use.

Silicone rubber molds will withstand high temperatures—high enough that you can pour melted picco resins (400°F.) into them. And that's pretty hot.

Safety Considerations

Silicone RTV resins are less destructive than those you will encounter when you work with urethanes or polyester. The catalyst is also more stable and less dangerous, but this is like saying that one poison is less deadly than another.

Care must be exercised when you work with any harmful materials. Silicone is moderately toxic by skin contact. The catalyst is harmful to both skin and eye tissue.

SUMMARY: Wear latex gloves and goggles when mixing and pouring silicone.

RTV—Room Temperature Vulcanizing

Charles Goodyear discovered vulcanization in 1835, when he accidentally spilled a latex compound on his stove. The heat cured the rubber, making it strong and resistant to changes in temperature.

The technology has advanced in the last 150 years. You will meet two kinds of synthetic rubber in this book that will vulcanize when a catalyst is added, and at room temperature. We are about to discuss one—a mold-making material, silicone RTV; the other, urethane RTV, is used for making flexible castings.

Cost Reduction

Silicone RTV rubber is expensive. A gallon kit of silicone retails for about $75.00 at this writing. It is clear that you cannot use silicone in the same carefree manner that plaster is used. Plaster is cheap; silicone is costly. But this problem is one that people have been working on. You may be pleased to know that techniques have been developed which make silicone more economical and within reach of any producing company's budget.

• Silicone can be reinforced with stretch fabrics, making it stronger in thin layers.

• Mother molds of plaster surrounding thin cross-sections of silicone rubber support it while castings are made.

• A technique of controlling wall thickness of the mold by injecting silicone into a preformed plaster shell has become standard.

• Fillers have been found which can extend the volume of silicone, making it less costly per cubic inch.

Each of these techniques will be demonstrated in the following pages.

Fabric Reinforcements

One way of keeping the walls of a silicone mold thin and strong is to reinforce the rubber with a cloth that will stretch in at least one direction. A mold made in this manner will use little material and be economical. This is a very useful process to know and use, even if you are not interested in reproducing a walking stick.

Prepare the pattern — in this case a real walking stick handle — by removing it from the cane, cleaning it of all dirt, grease, and contaminants, and mounting it on a base.

No mold release is necessary. (None ever is with silicone RTV.)

Mix up a small batch (80 ml — about 2½ fl. oz.) of silicone according to the instructions on the can.

The silicone used in these photos can be mixed either by weight or volume to a ratio of 10:1. Measure out 80 ml of rubber and 8 ml of the cata-

lyst. Stir the mixture thoroughly. The silicone is white, and the catalyst is violet. The color difference is very helpful in knowing when the job of stirring is completed. Just keep stirring the mixture till it is a uniform pastel shade of the catalyst color.

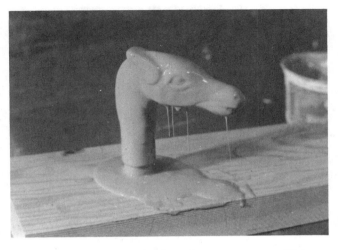

Ladle this mixture onto the pattern. This first application, known as an impression coat, needs to be thorough, covering all parts of the model. This coating can be thin as long as it is complete.

The silicone is so liquid and runny, you will have trouble making a thick coating stay in place. Leave the unit alone for an hour or so and it will begin to thicken and become a little more manageable.

Scoop some of the puddle off the base and re-apply it to the top of the pattern. This time a little more silicone will adhere to the surface. Do this three times with one-hour waiting periods between coatings.

Let the pattern remain undisturbed to cure overnight.

Fast-Setting Catalysts

There are silicone rubbers on the market that have two catalysts: one considered to be standard, and one which is fast setting. When the fast catalyst is used, the set-up time of the rubber can be as little as ten minutes. This faster combination is good for making cloth lay-up and impression coats.

After the impression layer has cured, the process of reinforcing this layer begins. Use a loose weave cloth, one that has some flex in its fibers and will stretch. The weave must also be open so that the silicone can soak completely through the fabric. Cheesecloth is a fabric of this kind. Jersey is good, so is Spandex. The photo shows the use of a loose weave nylon which has a lot of flexibility.

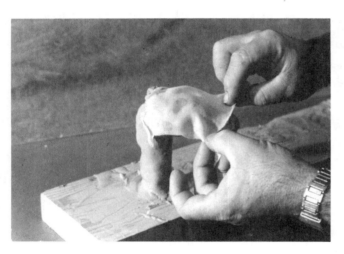

Paint a fresh application of catalyzed silicone on to the pattern. If it is mixed with a standard catalyst (such as we are using in the illustrations) it will tend to be unmanageable. Cut a small patch of cloth and lay it onto the wetted pattern. The silicone will soak into the fibers and become much more controllable. Keep adding patches, overlapping them at their edges, till the entire pattern is covered with two coats of cloth. Where the pieces overlap it is possible that some areas are built up to a depth of four or more layers.

Scrape the silicone off your clean table surface and reapply it to the fabric-coated pattern. The soaking of the silicone into the cloth should hold it in place and keep it from slouching all over your work space. Give the pattern a second overnight curing period.

The silicone mold is almost finished. It is economical in terms of material but, it must be admitted, costly in terms of waiting time. You must decide which is more dear to your production needs.

Mother Molds

The walls of a silicone mold, strengthened with layers of cloth, are about 1/8″ to 3/16″ thick. With walls this thin the mold is excessively flexible and must be surrounded with a firm material to ensure that the true shape of the original is retained.

This reinforcement is usually a plaster *mother mold*. Its construction is an extra step in the mold-making process, but when you are using silicone rubber in thin cross-sections, it is a necessary one.

Plaster reinforcements are easy to make and it will not take much more time. This one was made by pouring plaster into a well-greased box and gently forcing the silicone-coated pattern down halfway into the plaster.

We spoke against the technique of pushing objects into wet plaster earlier as we demonstrated how to construct good quality plaster molds, but mother molds are another matter. Small air bubbles may collect on the underside of the silicone, but small air bubbles are not a matter of great concern when you are making a mother mold.

When the plaster has set up to butter consistency and begins to get warm, dig out some keying depressions with a coin.

As soon as the lower half of the plaster surround has cooled off the top half can be poured. Coat the plaster surface with liquid soap or petroleum jelly so the plaster will release cleanly from the bottom portion.

It's O.K. to pour the top half of the plaster mold without benefit of wooden side boards if you work patiently, adding plaster to the mold by the handfuls as the plaster progressively thickens. This technique has been explained in the section on making a One-Part Plaster Mold (pages 37 to 39). When the plaster becomes workable, just scrape it with a putty knife, making it conform to the wooden box lying underneath.

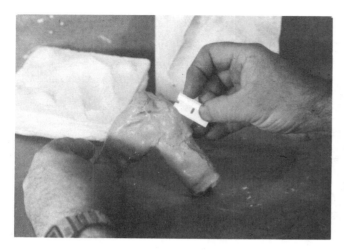

Cut a slit down the back of the mold to release the original pattern from the silicone. Use a new sharp razor blade to make this slit as clean as possible.

The mother mold is cut on a band saw to expose the throat of the silicone material and provide a sprue for pouring the casting material.

This silicone mold is now ready to use for making castings. The resilience of the silicone rubber will snap the mold shut when it is released, and the plaster mother mold will hold it tightly in this position.

These photos have been included to finish the story. They show a casting being made from this mold with Water Extendable Polyester. See

Water Extendable Polyester (WEP) in the section on casting materials (pages 145 and 146) for the details on how to use this material.

Making an Injected Silicone Rubber Mold

In the description that follows, the mother mold is made first — before the silicone mold is poured. This plaster shell will be made leaving a carefully calculated space between the pattern and the plaster mother mold. You will then be instructed to inject silicone rubber into the cavity. A silicone mold thus formed will have thin walls of a precisely planned thickness.

To demonstrate this technique, two items are shown under construction: a "high-tech" telephone and a decorative wall bracket for a wall sconce.

The telephone receiver will be built into a box form — this process was detailed earlier, in making the mold of the fish (pages 30 to 36). The wall bracket will use the method demonstrated in molding the casket hardware (pages 37 to 39).

Both systems will be illustrated at the same time to show more clearly how you might approach silicone mold-making techniques.

Measure the model so it can be fitted with a box. This telephone will need a box with inside dimensions of about 5″ × 11″.

Anchoring the Pattern

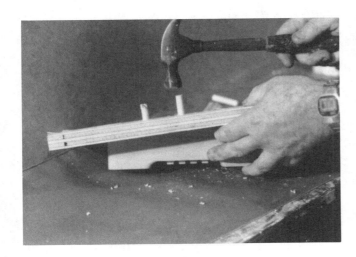

The pattern that you wish to duplicate must be anchored firmly to a base. The telephone and its base have been drilled and joined with wooden pegs. The bracket is held in place with a ¼″ lag screw.

When the plaster mother mold is made, it too will be secured to the base. The alignment between the pattern and the mother mold will thus remain constant, and the cavity formed between these walls will remain certain and accurate.

Applying a Clay Space Saver

Cover the pattern with a coating of wax-based modeling clay. Do not be overly concerned with pressing the clay into all of the details and crevices of the pattern; just make a blanket of Plasticine about ¼" thick. The clay is acting as a "space saver" as the plaster mother mold is being made. If you make these clay walls thicker, the silicone mold will be thicker—perhaps thicker than necessary. But then, if you make them too thin, the silicone mold may not hold its shape. Try to keep this blanket about ¼" thick.

It is extremely important that you do not use oil-based clay anywhere near silicone. The same art store that sells oil-based modeling clays will also handle the wax-based product.

Pictured here you see the telephone receiver wrapped in its blanket of wax-base clay. The sides have been given a slight taper. Any time you can make the side walls of a mold sloping rather than straight, it facilitates an easier separation.

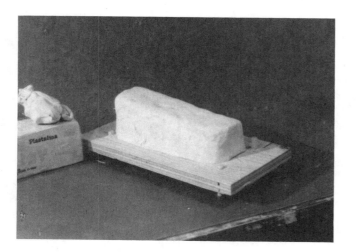

Pegging the Base for Perfect Alignment

Locate and drill two holes in opposite corners of the base. Insert wooden pegs in these holes, allowing them to project about ½" into the interior of the box. When the plaster is poured, these pegs will act as keying devices keeping the mother mold aligned with reference to the pattern. Don't forget to coat the pegs and box with petroleum jelly.

Pouring the Mother Mold

Pour plaster over the clay-blanketed pattern. Tap the box with a hammer to dislodge air bubbles. Actually, any flaws caused by air bubbles forming on the surface of this mother mold will cause no trouble. The purpose of this plaster is just to hold the silicone shell in place.

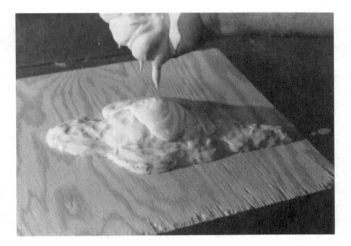

To prepare a one-piece mother mold, mix the plaster for the wall sconce to a somewhat thicker pouring consistency and apply it patiently to the mold. Pat the first application all over the pattern with your fingers to make an impression coating.

When the plaster gets to butter consistency, you can smooth out the roughness of its exterior and make it more presentable.

When you pour a mother mold without benefit of a box, you must be patient, piling the plaster onto the pattern ever higher, as the thickening mixture allows. If the plaster runs a little, scoop it back up onto the pile.

Drilling Alignment Holes
(Alternate Method)

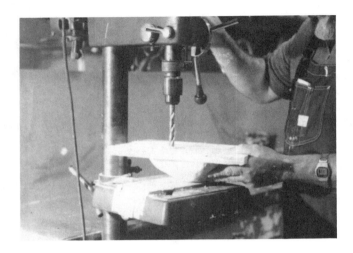

The plaster mother mold for the wall bracket must now be drilled and fitted with wooden plugs. These plugs act as keying devices to hold the parts in alignment in the steps that follow. You will remember that the telephone receiver was drilled and plugged *before* the plaster was poured. These are two options that can be used. Neither way is necessarily better.

Saving the Wad of Clay

When the plaster hardens and the keying plugs have been secured, you can separate the mold

parts and remove, wad up, and save the clay.

It becomes immediately obvious that the wall sconce will use about one-third less silicone than the telephone receiver. The wad of clay you have removed represents the exact volume of the cavity.

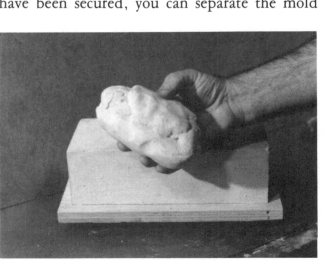

Using it as an aid, you can easily mix the proper amount of liquid rubber needed to refill either of these spaces.

Drilling Sprues

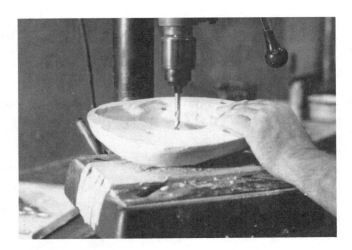

Drill holes (called "sprues") into the plaster mother mold. Silicone will be slowly injected into these sprues, replacing the air in the cavity, to make the rubber mold. Study the face of your pattern to find its lowest depressions. A sprue should be drilled directly over each of these places to assure the injected rubber reaches the deep concavity and that no air pockets form. Then drill other sprues—as many as you judge are necessary to accommodate your pattern. We used five holes for the wall bracket and three for the telephone, but your piece might require more or possibly less. Drill one final hole in the apex of your mold. This is an air hole, which allows air to escape as you inject silicone into the lower sprues.

There will be evidence of these sprues in the finished silicone mold, but that's O.K.—they will be on its backside. The face of the mold will contain the unblemished shape of the pattern.

Aligning the Mother Mold over the Pattern

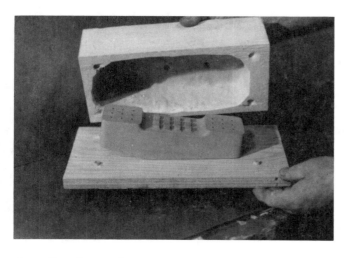

Clean away all of the chips and debris that are left as a result of the drilling, and refit the mother mold onto the keyed platform over the original pattern. This will make a cavity with uniform walls completely surrounding the pattern. Clamp the mother mold firmly to the base with restraints —bungie cord, circles of rubber cut from an innertube, or strap clamps.

Any freedom of movement might allow the injected rubber to seep out between the mold and the wooden base. It is sometimes helpful to seal this union by forcing a small amount of water-based clay into the seam where they meet.

Please note that we will not use a mold release as we continue—none is needed when you make a mold of silicone.

Mixing the Silicone RTV

Everything is now ready, so we can mix the silicone. Set your scale so it balances with the empty container. In the example illustrated, the empty jar weighs seven ounces.

Remember that wad of clay we saved? Work it in your hands until its diameter approximates that of your mixing container. This wad of clay is a very good indication of how much silicone is needed to fill the mold. However, now that you *know* how much is needed and you are not guessing, mix a little extra. Do not be stingy with your materials. If you don't mix enough, the whole mold can be ruined, and there is no economy in that.

Fill the jar with silicone rubber to the desired volume and then weigh it. Don't forget to subtract the weight of the empty container. The liquid rubber we used for the lamp bracket mold weighed about eight ounces. The rubber for the telephone mold weighed about twenty-six ounces.

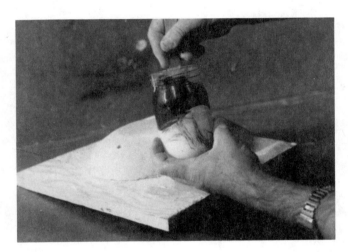

The product we are using needs to be mixed to a ratio of one part (by weight) of catalyst to ten parts (by weight) of liquid silicone. For the wall bracket mold, the scale was set up 0.8 oz. (to 8.8 oz.) and we poured the catalyst into the jar till the scale balanced with this weight.

Stir your mixture thoroughly.

There is no need to rush—you have plenty of time to mix the catalyst into the silicone completely. It will take at least an hour for this mixture to show any signs of thickening. Try not to whip any air into the mixture.

Preventing Air Bubbles with a Vacuum Chamber

When silicone rubber is used by those who take full advantage of its reproductive fineness, as in medical processes or in criminal investigations, the blend is submitted to a vacuum to remove all of the air that might have been trapped in the liquid. If you are doing exacting work and have a vacuum chamber—use it. The rest of us will just have to use the mixture as is.

Injecting the Silicone RTV

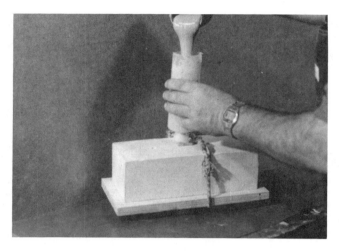

Pour the mixture into a syringe and inject it through the sprues. In the photo of the telephone mold (above left) our syringe is a white glue dispenser that has had its bottom cut away. The lamp bracket mold is being filled with a syringe purchased from a hobby shop.

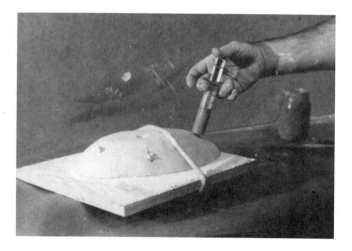

It takes two hands to make a glue bottle operate as a syringe. You must cover the open end with one hand and squeeze the bottle with the other. The one-hand operation of the manufactured syringe is much more convenient. Inject the silicone repeatedly into the sprues. Work around the mold, squirting the liquid into all of the low areas located under the sprues.

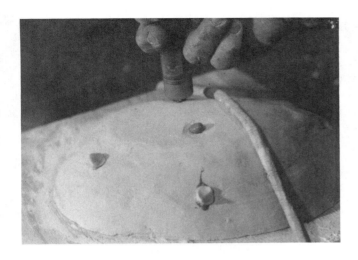

As you continue to inject the liquid into the mold, air will be forced out of the adjacent sprues and, of course, out of the top air hole. As the silicone level rises, liquid will begin to flow out of the sprues. When this happens, the holes should be plugged with *wax-based* or *water-based* modeling clay. If you detect leakage between the mold and the plywood base, rub clay into the joint to stop the flow.

Continue filling the mold till the top air vent begins to ooze with the liquid rubber. Keep an eye on this vent. As the air bubbles come to the surface through this hole, you must give another shot through the syringe to keep the mold full to overflowing.

The Finished Mold

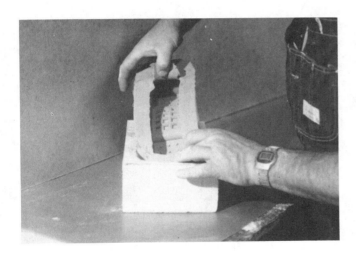

Allow the rubber to cure overnight. You will be able to peel the rubber shell from the pattern and its base, releasing the silicone mold. This mold and its plaster mother mold are ready for immediate use.

Extending Silicone with Fillers

The high cost of silicone RTV has prompted certain craftsmen to improve on its economy by developing fillers which will extend the volume of silicone without increasing its price. Procedures have been devised using Cab-O-Sil and ground silicone rubber. Adding fillers to the silicone is a little like adding extra carrots and potatoes to the stew when unexpected relatives drop in at meal time. It dilutes the stew, changes the flavor a little, but it makes the stew go a lot further.

A lion head door knocker has been chosen as a project to demonstrate the use of recycled silicone as a filler.

This lion head has been sculpted from wax-based modeling clay and was shown in the section on The Model (page 23); the technique of making the castings from Dowman's Fixall will be demonstrated in the section on Hardware Store Products (pages 173 and 174). The construction of the mold itself is shown here.

Again, please be cautioned against sculpting your model with an oil-based clay that can inhibit the cure of the silicone rubber.

The Impression Coating

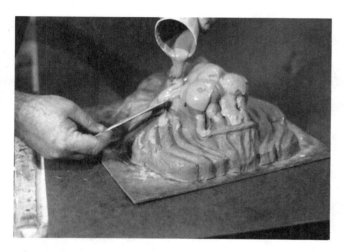 

Mix up some silicone according to the instructions outlined in the preceding sections, and heed the directions provided on the package accompanying your product. Measure carefully — do not guess.

Apply the stirred mixture onto your pattern to make an impression coat. For good results, it is important that this first coating (no matter how thin it might be) covers the whole model with a skin of pure unadulterated silicone. The silicone will do everything in its power to squander itself all over your table. Collect the drippings, putting them where you want them — back onto the model.

Allow this first coating an undisturbed four to five hours to cure and become tacky to the touch. An impression layer made mid-morning will be firm enough to continue working with in mid-afternoon.

Recycling Silicone Rubber

Silicone doesn't stick to anything (we've been bragging about how a mold release is never necessary), but it will stick to itself! A filler made by grating an old discarded silicone mold and mixing the grindings with liquid rubber can more than double the working volume of your silicone.

Cut an old silicone mold into "bite size" pieces with a band saw or with a serrated knife blade. Run these chunks through a meat grinder. You should be able to make fragments about the size of split peas or popcorn kernels on this first grinding.

Run the "kernels" through the grinder again, and you will have granules the size of coffee grounds or bird seed.

If you add two ounces of these silicone grindings to two ounces of catalyzed silicone liquid rubber, you will have almost four ounces of pure silicone —chunk style.

Spread the batter over the impression coating with a cake knife—in fact, you will find this procedure to be a lot like icing a cake. The thick mix is a lot easier to control than unfilled silicone, but it still responds to the effects of gravity and needs to be attended to. Spread it back up onto the form until the rubber begins to stiffen.

Let the silicone cure for about twelve hours.

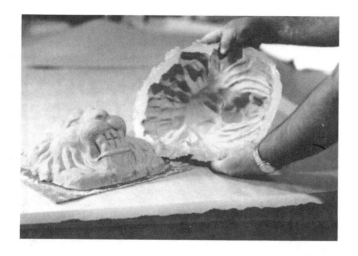

The mold will release from the pattern with no difficulty. The walls are very flexible and will separate from the pattern's undercuts inflicting no damage to the clay sculpture. However, even though the wall of the mold is built up to a thickness of ½″ to ¾″, it cannot hold its shape under the pressure of its own weight. Typically, a silicone mold must be backed up with plaster.

Restore the correct shape of the silicone mold by again fitting it over the pattern.

Constructing a Two-Part Mother Mold

Sometimes (as in the case of this lion head), the silicone mold will have undercuts even in its exterior surface. The mother mold then must be made in two parts. A two-part mother mold easily falls away from the silicone mold, freeing it to separate from the more pronounced undercuts present in either the sculpted pattern or the castings it produces.

Build up a clay wall on the exterior of the silicone mold, directly on its center line, dividing the mold surface in equal halves. The clay wall will define the thickness of the mother mold and set the seam line where the halves of this two-part mold will separate.

Now that the silicone has cured, any clay can be used. The oil-based clay that was such a threat to wet silicone has no ill effects on cured silicone or plaster.

Reinforcing Plaster with Cheesecloth

Mix up a half gallon batch of plaster according to the procedure outlined in the section on Mixing Plaster (pages 32 and 33). During the waiting period while the plaster is soaking up its required moisture, cut three or four sections of cheesecloth about a foot square.

Dip the cheesecloth in the plaster. Lay the saturated cloth on the surface of the silicone mold, smoothing it down and coaxing it to lie as close as possible to this shape. Dip each of the pieces of cheesecloth in turn, and overlap them as they are applied.

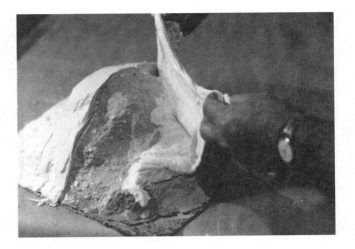

Smooth the edge that falls along the clay wall, ensuring that it forms a flat surface for a good fit when the second half of the mother mold is mated to it. Finally, use a putty knife to smooth the exterior surface of the mother mold and shape it to conform to the thickness of the clay wall.

The use of cheesecloth allows you some control over the free-flowing plaster, constraining it from sliding off the form. It is also one of several reinforcing materials which allow you to build up a plaster wall that is strong even though it has a thin cross-section. Since we have not bothered to make an impression coating, the surface between the silicone and the plaster will be flawed, per-

haps containing air bubbles or evidence of the rough texture of the cheesecloth, but these flaws are not a matter of concern when they occur in a mother mold.

When the plaster has cured, pull away the clay wall. The silicone surface needs no mold release, but the exposed plaster surface does. Use some liquid soap or petroleum jelly so the second half of the mold will separate cleanly after it is cast.

Mix up another small batch of plaster and cut four more pieces of cheesecloth. Apply them just as you did in the previous operation.

Clamping a Two-Part Plaster Mother Mold

A multi-part mold must be bound together with a clamp or restraining band of some kind. It is sometimes necessary to build little bumps into the surface of the plaster's exterior to keep these bands from sliding off of the tapered sides. The bumps in the mold shown in the photo are made from ½" washers which have been embedded in a fresh coating of plaster with the aid of a small wad of plaster-saturated cheesecloth.

Assemble the mold pieces and hold them together with a clamp or restraint. Strap clamps, as illustrated in the photo on the left, are available in large sizes at hardware stores. As these clamps are tightened, they will pull the seam tightly together.

Silicone molds can be used to cast almost any casting material except those requiring plaster absorption: slip clay and neoprene. This head can be cast with polyester resins, foam urethane, urethane RTV, latex, any member of the plaster family, and most of the hot melts. You can follow the career of this mold by turning to the section on Hardware Store Products (pages 173 and 174) and see a casting made with a commercial patching plaster.

MOLD RELEASES

If you work through the list of casting products demonstrated in this book, you will find that some of them are either naturally releasing, or that the water present in the mold acts as a mold release.

Many of the plastic molding and casting materials, however, have a tendency to stick to each other. The same stuff that "Company A" is compounding and selling as casting resin, "Company B" is compounding and selling as a super glue. If you pour a plastic resin, with all its great characteristics as a casting material, into a mold and it adheres to the sides of the form, you can't blame the chemicals. They don't know any better. They think they are *supposed* to grab onto anything they come in contact with; after all, it's one of the tricks they were bred to perform. In order to use an adhesive product as a casting material, something has to be done to curb this tendency of the chemicals to hold

fast. The mold-making engineers decided that the best way to solve this problem was to provide a film of some kind (a mold release) which, when applied to the mold, would protect it from the molecular grip of the casting material. Several such releases—based in wax, grease, or soap—have long been known, seeing use in the days of plaster, papier-mâché, and Celastic. These release agents—detergent, paste floor wax, paraffin, petroleum jelly, and mineral oil—were tried, with varying degrees of success, on the new plastics.

The chemists found that just as some plastics (epoxies, caseins, and urethanes) stick to almost everything, others (polyethylene, vinyl, fluorocarbon [Teflon], and silicone) develop impervious skins to which almost nothing will stick. On page 80 you will find a chart listing twenty casting materials and the recommended mold-releasing agents.

Self-Releasing Molds

Several of the products listed are naturally non-sticking and require no additional mold release. Alginate, hot melt rubber, and silicone casting rubber will release from almost any casting material. This characteristic puts them in high favor as mold-making materials.

Absorption Molds

The materials that work on the absorption principle of slip casting (slip clay, latex, neoprene rubber) work with a plaster mold and require no mold release. In fact, if the mold is not dry and absolutely clean of wax, grease, or any other contaminant that might seal the absorption properties of the plaster, the process will not work.

Water as a Release Agent

Plastic wood and the polyolefins—polyethylene and polypropylene—will not stick to a moist surface. Hot glue is one of these, and will release cleanly from a surface porous enough to hold a fair amount of water. Plaster molds work well with these casting materials if the mold has been soaked in water for three to four minutes before use.

Aluminum Foil

Sometimes a thin layer of aluminum foil can be pressed into a mold and used as a parting agent. You will lose a fair amount of detail using this process, and this must be taken into account; but at times when some fineness of detail can be sacrificed, foil is a reasonable option.

Petroleum Jelly, Green Soap, and Wax

Celastic, papier-mâché, and all of the forms of gypsum plaster release from nonporous surfaces thinly coated with petroleum jelly, soap, or wax. Porous surfaces require a heavier coating.

Petroleum jelly is the non-trademark name for Vaseline.

Tincture of green soap is the soap-based mold releasing product that tradition has handed down to us. You can make up a batch of this soapy mold release, if you'd like, by shaving a block of laundry soap into a quart of water and heating it (do not boil) till the soap chips are dissolved. If you are not a slave to tradition, liquid dish-washing detergent also works very well.

You can prepare a wax-based release agent by thinning paste floor wax to a thick liquid with kerosene. This solution can be applied with a brush and is easier to handle than the same wax in paste form.

If it seems that the separation is going to be difficult, as would be the case in making a plaster cast in a plaster mold, there is an advantage in using two releasing agents—soap and wax—on the same mold.

Coat the mold with the liquid soap, allow it to dry, and then coat it again with the liquid paste wax. Allow this to dry and then make the casting.

Although the wax can be smoothly applied to the soaped surface, the two release agents are not compatible: wax will not adhere to the soapy film. The mold does not stick to the soap, the casting does not adhere to the wax, and the wax and the soap do not cling. Separation is impeded only by a rough surface or undercuts.

As I started working with polyester resins in the late 1950s, a heavy coat of shellac and a thin coat of petroleum jelly were recommended by some manufacturers (as much as they would recommend anything) as a parting agent between a plaster mold and polyester–fiberglass casting. The combination worked and it still does, if you don't mind the slight side effect. The oil-based petroleum jelly will slightly inhibit the cure of the surface skin of the polyester. When you pull such a casting from the mold, the surface which was touching the greased mold must be sanded because of its roughened skin. If you want to eliminate this sanding step (and for mass production this is essential), don't use petroleum jelly as a release agent.

PVA

Polyester resins that require catalysts, urethane two-part foams, and the urethane rubbers that vulcanize at room temperature are the ones that think they are adhesives, so the surfaces they come in contact with must be specially treated. Polyvinyl alcohol, or PVA, is a widely used mold release today for these casting materials. It is a vinyl plastic suspended in an alcohol base. You brush or spray this mold release onto a smooth mold surface, and as the alcohol dries away, a thin coating of vinyl is left behind. The skin can be built up with repeated applications of PVA, allowing sufficient drying time between the coatings.

If you must cast fiberglass in a plaster mold, it must be sealed with some sort of paint, either sprayed or brushed onto the surface of the mold to make it less porous. Lacquer or vinyl paints can be used successfully. The sealed surface must then be coated with mold release. Fiberglass castings (if they are large or intricate) can be very tricky. Waxing the sealer, dusting it with talc, then applying PVA with an airbrush works well. The talc helps keep the PVA from pulling the sealer off the plaster when the separation is troublesome.

Plaster molds are *not* recommended when you are casting with aggressively tenacious plastic materials. Silicone RTV molds are best, because they are flexible, give high resolution, and are naturally releasing.

The rigid two-part urethane foam is the most tenacious of the group and should always be cast in a silicone mold. When circumstances force you to use a plaster mold, your casting always requires a sealant, PVA, paste wax, and talcum powder—and you can still resign yourself to a high probability of failure.

Glass as a Mold Release

Polyester resin will not stick to the smooth hard surface of clean glass! You can make a fiberglass casting if you have such a mold and if there are no undercuts present in the mold, without any other mold release. Likewise, a fiberglass mold could be made from a clean glass pattern.

Other Release Factors

Always make it a rule to cast a *hard* material (plaster, polyester resin, fiberglass, etc.) in a flexible or *soft* mold, to allow an easy release. A soft or flexible mold peels away a little at a time and is so much easier to separate than one that must be ''popped'' apart all at one time. Undercuts are impossible unless this rule is followed.

Thin, laminated castings (papier-mâché, Celastic, fiberglass) are known to shrink a little (or a lot) and are most successfully cast in a negative mold, the shrinkage actually facilitating the release. It is reasonable, however, to make a carefully crafted laminated casting from a positive mold if it is loosened just prior to its total cure. In fact, it can be considered to be flexible while in this state. Once the seal is broken, the casting can be returned to the mold, allowing the cure to complete. If compressed air is available, jets of air directed between the laminated skin and the positive mold are sometimes helpful. All these precautions are particularly important if there are any undercuts present in the mold, even the smallest ones.

Mold Release Recommendations

CASTING MATERIAL	PLASTER MOLD	ALGINATE MOLD	LATEX MOLD	SILICONE MOLD	GLASS OR METAL MOLD
MATERIALS USING THE ABSORPTION PROCESS:					
Slip Clay	No release needed	*Not recommended*	*Not recommended*	*Not recommended*	*Not recommended*
Neoprene	No release needed	*Not recommended*	*Not recommended*	*Not recommended*	*Not recommended*
Latex	No release needed	*Not recommended*	PVA and wax	No release needed	No release needed
MATERIALS IN THE HOT MELT FAMILY:					
Wax (paraffin)	*Not recommended*	*Not recommended*	No release needed	No release needed	*Not recommended*
Hot melt rubber	No release needed	*Not recommended*	No release needed	No release needed	No release needed
Hot melt glue	Dip mold in water	*Not recommended*	*Not recommended*	No release needed	*Not recommended*
Hot modeling clay (wax based)	*Not recommended*	*Not recommended*	No release needed	No release needed	*Not recommended*
MATERIALS OF THE PLASTER FAMILY:					
Plaster	Petroleum jelly or green soap or liquid wax	No release needed	No release needed	No release needed	Petroleum jelly or green soap
Fix-all	Petroleum jelly or soap	No release needed	No release needed	No release needed	Petroleum jelly or soap
Durham's Rockhard	Petroleum jelly or soap	No release needed	No release needed	No release needed	Petroleum jelly or soap
SOME MISCELLANEOUS CASTING MATERIALS:					
Papier-Mache	Petroleum jelly or soap	*Not recommended*	*Not recommended*	No release needed	Petroleum jelly or soap
Celastic	Petroleum jelly or soap	*Not recommended*	*Not recommended*	No release needed	Petroleum jelly or soap
Plastic Wood	Dip mold in water	*Not recommended*	*Not recommended*	No release needed	*Not recommended*
MATERIALS IN THE POLYESTER RESIN FAMILY:					
Polyester casting resin	Lacquer, PVA, talc, PVA, and wax	*Not recommended*	PVA and wax	No release needed	No release needed on glass
Fiberglass	Lacquer, PVA, talc, PVA, and wax	*Not recommended*	PVA	No release needed	Light coat of petroleum jelly
WEP	Lacquer, PVA, and wax	No release needed	No release needed	No release needed	Light coat of petroleum jelly
MATERIALS MADE OF POLYURETHANE PLASTICS:					
Urethane RTV	Lacquer, PVA, talc, PVA, and wax	*Not recommended*	PVA, talc, PVA, and wax	No release needed	PVA, talc, PVA, and wax
Urethane foams	Lacquer, PVA, talc, PVA, and wax	*Not recommended*	PVA, talc, PVA, and wax	No release needed	PVA, talc, PVA, and wax

MAKING THE CASTINGS

Choosing the Right Casting Material

There are several things to think about as you select the right casting material for any given project. You will, of course, be concerned with the strength and durability of the casting. Weight is frequently a factor—not only the weight of the casting itself but also the weight of associated trappings and special effects requirements. The selection of the casting material can have a great influence on the finished look of the object. Don't neglect the economy considerations of your project in terms of both material costs and time. And finally (perhaps it should be your *first* consideration), you must be aware of the dangers of the material you want to use and determine whether you are equipped to do the job safely.

Strength of the Casting

In deciding how durable any property is to be, you must know how much use the item will receive and how many performances the show will run. Then, you must decide if you want the item to last just the run of the show or whether it should be built for stock. If the cast object is to be a decorative wall hanging where there is no risk of damage, it can be made of papier-mâché; if there is to be a great deal of business with it, perhaps you should make it more durable, casting it in Celastic; and if you want to keep it in stock for other productions you might think about casting it in fiberglass.

You could also ask yourself whether it might be prudent to take a chance building the prop of a less durable material and repairing it if and when that becomes necessary.

Weight of the Finished Casting

Is the weight of the finished casting important? Does it require easy manipulation? Will it have to accommodate any electronics, mechanics, magic? Is the product strong enough, or is the material too bulky to mount these special requirements? Must it break away, and will the casting material allow this feature?

The Finished Look

Several of the casting materials have a natural sheen which might be to your advantage. There are problems encountered when you try to color some of the plastics—urethanes, styrenes, latex, and ethylenes. If the prop needs to be translucent or transparent your choices are probably limited to the polyester resins. Some of the casting materials have a dull finish that can be smoothed with sanding, but that requires extra time.

Economy—Costs of Materials and Labor

The costs of materials can be calculated relatively easily, and most of them are inexpensive. Many of the techniques of molding and casting are time consuming, and your cost in terms of hours spent on a project is not always obvious. Until you become experienced with a particular process you will nearly always underestimate how much time the procedure will take. The time you spend in set-up and clean-up will vary a lot depending on which materials you use. The same is true of time allowed to trim, smooth, and color the completed castings.

Availability of Product

Is the project a rush job? Is the product you choose locally available or will you have to special order it from a distant city? It even takes a certain amount of time to run across town to pick up a product you want and do not have in stock. (Especially if you forget some item and have to make the trip twice.)

Safety Considerations

After you have considered all the preceding factors and have tentatively selected a material, check to see whether you have the knowledge and special safety equipment (exhaust fans, fume hoods, goggles, respirators, gloves, aprons, and confidence) the process requires. *If you cannot perform the necessary steps safely, choose another material!*

Physical and Chemical Incompatibilities

This consideration is dealt with in more detail in the section on mold releases, but it might be wise to list some of the major problems again here.

1. Any mold made for slipcasting must be free of contamination — petroleum jelly.

2. A mold made for use with polyester resins must be free of moisture and petroleum jelly.

3. Silicone molds cannot be made in the presence of oil-based modeling clay.

4. Latex deteriorates rapidly in the presence of petroleum products.

5. Hard, rigid casting materials separate with great difficulty from hard, rigid molds.

This list is not complete, and you will become aware of other incompatible chemicals and techniques and learn how to work with them as you gain experience. But compatibility is a consideration when selecting casting materials.

Negative and Positive Forms

Your pattern or model is considered to be a ''positive'' shape. A bump or raised design is truly raised and stands out in relief in a realistic way.

A casting taken from this pattern is considered to be ''negative.'' All of the three-dimensional relief is reversed in the casting. A bump appears as a depression, and a pit is preserved in the casting as a bulge.

A casting taken from a negative mold will again be positive.

ABSORPTION CASTING

Absorption casting is a very old pottery-making technique in which liquid clay (called *slip*) is poured into a plaster mold. The dry plaster mold absorbs water from the liquid clay, building a fragile wall inside the mold. This wall remains behind when the clay is poured out. It is allowed to dry a little more, and then is removed from the mold and fired in a kiln to make a finished casting. Slip clay, latex, and neoprene will be explained on the next few pages as the slipcasting process is demonstrated.

Slipcasting

In William Gibson's *The Miracle Worker,* a milk pitcher must be broken each night that the play runs—a piece of business necessary to the action of the play. In Jeff Brown's *Family Matters,* a frightened child drops and breaks a flower vase. In Chekhov's *The Three Sisters,* an heirloom clock is accidentally knocked to the floor and smashed—nightly.

Slipcasting is one of several ways that this sort of stage effect may be provided. Far and away the simplest way is to buy enough copies of the required prop, consider them expendable, and break them. This is not, however, the most dependable method. Too often, a store-bought item, even if it is made of glass, will bounce when it is supposed to break on cue. Of course, when it does break, you have another problem—the sharp shards of glass are dangerous.

Then there is the matter of expense. Fifteen to twenty breakaway copies might have to be ob-tained to have enough to supply a production's two-week run and its necessary dress rehearsals. Heirloom clocks or even milk pitchers become large budgetary concerns for a small producing company when purchased in these quantities.

Making a plaster mold and reproducing these props in slipcasting is more economical in terms of money, but it must be admitted up front that you will have to make a large investment in terms of time. It takes about a week and a half from the time you select the model you want copied till you have twenty slipcastings completed, fired, and ready for paint. I hasten to point out that much of this period is time spent waiting for the castings to dry. If, however, you already have a ready-to-use plaster mold in your possession, the time can almost be cut in half.

It is important to know, if you are going to do slipcastings, that you must plan ahead and budget your time.

Making the Plaster Mold

The techniques of making a plaster mold are covered in the section on plaster casting. Since this mold is made very much the same as the ones described there, reference will only be made here to the special problems that you might encounter in casting a milk pitcher such as is called for in *The Miracle Worker.*

Preparing the Pattern

Choose a pitcher made of smooth glass or stainless steel to use as a pattern for making the slipcast reproductions. The pitcher illustrated was selected because it has a good size and shape, and because the steel surface will make a very smooth finish on the plaster mold.

Eliminate all undercuts that you can find in the pattern with an application of Plasticine. The depression in the pitcher's base was the only undercut that we found in this pattern.

The handle, however, was too thin where it met the body of the pitcher, and we built it up with modeling clay so the reproductions would have more strength at this point. The metal lip was also too thin to have any strength in a slipcast copy. This lip was built up with modeling clay at the same time that the mouth of the pitcher was plugged.

Begin making a wall of Plasticine around the pitcher that leaves just half of the pattern exposed. Continue the wall till the pitcher is completely surrounded.

Make a large box that has a clearance of at least one inch between the pattern and its sides. Use liquid soap as a mold release*. Rub it onto the surface of the pitcher and all of the wooden parts of the box. All areas must be covered, but be careful not to use too much. A very thin coating is sufficient for the plaster to separate from the pattern.

*Petroleum jelly should not be used as a mold release when you are making a mold for slipcasting. Petroleum jelly can transfer to the plaster, clogging the pores and destroying the absorptive properties of the plaster.

Pouring the Plaster

It took about a gallon of mixed plaster to pour the mold for this pitcher. Casting plaster will work pretty well in this process, but #1 pottery plaster is designed for use in slipcasting and has better absorption properties.

You are now ready to pour the first half of a two-part mold. Pour the plaster into the mold and immediately begin tapping the sides of the box to shake loose air bubbles from the surface of the pattern.

Here is the first waiting period spoken of earlier. Allow the casting to set overnight so the plaster can harden, cure, and gain some strength.

Remove the box, turn the casting over, and remove the clay.

Using a large coin, scoop a couple of holes out of the soft plaster to provide keying. See the section on plaster casting for details on how this is done.

Reassemble the box and pour the second half of the mold. Wait overnight before removing the box and separating the mold halves.

Cut a wide hole into the mold right over the mouth of the pitcher, affording access to the interior of the mold. Fresh plaster cuts very easily with a saber saw.

When you cut fresh plaster with a file or a saw, you churn up a surprising amount of moisture, graphically illustrating the fact that there is a lot of water being held in the plaster crystals, and that there is need for a drying period before the mold can effectively be used as an absorption blotter in the slipcasting process.

If you start with a wet mold, maximum absorption will not be achieved, and the process cannot work efficiently. You should allow for a drying period of at least two days. Placing the mold in the sun or in a warm dry atmosphere aids the drying process.

And if the mold has been sitting idle for a very long time (over six months), it will probably be necessary to sponge the interior with water to add a little moisture. A very dry mold becomes *too* porous, and the casting may adhere to the plaster walls of the mold.

Safety Considerations

Happily, the materials used in slipcasting are much less hazardous than their relatives from the world of plastics. Slip clay is safest of all. Do not ingest the clay, and observe the precautions as outlined by the manufacturer of your kiln when working around this high-heat oven.

Making the Slipcasting

Working from the belief that two sets of pictures will tell a story more completely than one, the process of slipcasting will be illustrated with two simultaneous casting projects—the milk pitcher and a small flower vase. The construction of the mold for the vase was covered in the section on Two-Part Plaster Molds (pages 30 to 36).

Place the two halves of the mold together; the keys that have been built into the mold will keep the two halves in good alignment. Apply a restraint to keep them from coming apart. This restraint could be made from very large rubber bands or strips of rubber cut from automobile tire innertubes. (Do they still make innertubes?) Hardware stores stock strap clamps, and they work well, too. The clamps shown on the next page have been made from bungie cord.

Use low-fire slip. It can be purchased from a hobby shop or a potter's supply.

Pour the slip into the mold, filling it to the brim. Wait ten to fifteen minutes, and a wall about 3/16″ thick will form in all places where the slip touches the plaster. The longer you wait, the thicker this wall becomes. Watch to see if the level of the slip drops. It might be necessary to top off the slip as the water is absorbed into the mold.

After waiting the prescribed fifteen minutes, pour the surplus slip back into its jar. Wait another thirty minutes. This waiting period allows more moisture to be absorbed, and all the time the wall of your casting is gaining strength.

As the casting begins to dry, it shrinks ever so slightly, and it will begin to pull away from the plaster mold.

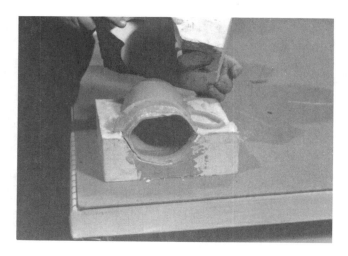

Gently rock the mold halves apart. Remove the top half of the mold. Take a look. Give the casting a gentle tug. You can now judge whether the casting has set up enough to be completely

withdrawn from the mold. If it needs more drying time, simply leave it alone and it will air dry, becoming stronger.

When you decide that it is ready, gently rock the casting to break it loose. The clay will still be soft and fragile, so be careful.

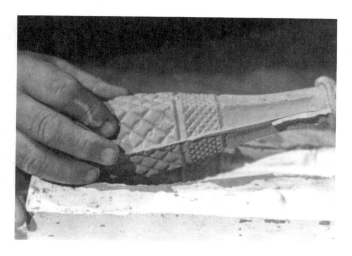

Lift the casting from its mold and gently set it onto its bottom. The clay will still be soft, and

the rounded bottom will push up into the vessel, forming a firm foundation at the base.

Trimming the Casting

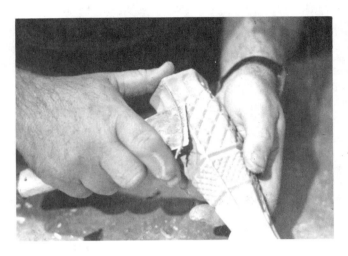

Work on the casting right away, trimming away imperfections while the clay is still soft.

Trim the seam line and then polish any raw edges with your dampened finger.

Firing the Casting

Set the clay casting aside for a couple more days before you fire it in a kiln. In an emergency (but *only* in an emergency) you can force-dry a slipcasting by putting it right into a small kiln, propping the door open a couple of inches, and setting the dial on low for an hour or so. Then fire the casting as described in the next step.

Bisque fire the dried casting in a small electric kiln. Load the casting into the kiln and heat it slowly to about 1500°F. Hold it there for a few hours and then turn the kiln off. Let the kiln and its contents rest undisturbed overnight while it cools. Your casting can be painted and it should be ready to drop to the stage floor for the breakage business.

If you fire the casting too much it will break in the kiln, and if you heat it too little it will be very fragile. Well, let's not lose sight of the fact that what we are after is a brittle, breakable article.

Ceramic artists do not like to think of degrees and minutes. They say that talking about the effects of heat working on clay for a certain amount of time is much too inaccurate. They have "cones" to monitor the effects of their kilns. If you can find one of these ceramic craftsmen, let him guide you. Otherwise, 1500°F. for a few hours should do it.

When you drop the pitcher, it will break. If the breakage seems to be too extensive, you can prepare the next pitcher with a coating of flex-glue before you break that one. This flexible coating will control some of the spatter.

Latex Casting

Two air-drying rubber products, latex and neoprene, work on the absorption casting process. Although latex and neoprene are both products based in rubber, they are not alike. There are a few similarities, but there are also some real differences. Latex is thicker initially; it takes longer to air dry; and, when cured, it remains more flexible than neoprene.

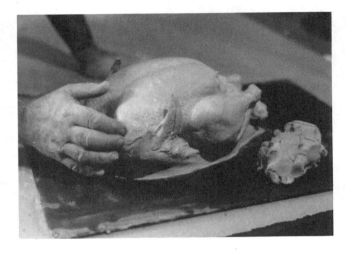

Our plaster mold was taken from a real turkey purchased from the supermarket. The model presented a few problem undercuts which were chinked with water-based clay applied directly onto the flesh of the bird.

Other undercuts could not be eliminated because they were deemed inherent to the true shape of the form. These undercuts were so extreme that the turkey had to be dissected in order to remove it from the plaster.

A mold release is not always necessary between a plaster mold and latex rubber. A little talcum powder can, however, be used to ensure easy separation if the mold has deep undercuts. Talcum powder does not in any way contaminate the mold or interfere with the curing of latex.

Safety Considerations

This product is not regarded as greatly hazardous. Latex rubber contains ammonia as a solvent, but the ammonia is not concentrated. Breathing a heavy concentration of ammonia vapors, however, can irritate your lungs and cause fluid to form there. Concentrated ammonia can also cause eye damage.

SUMMARY: Use latex in a space that has good general air movement.

Pouring the Latex Casting

Pour the plaster mold full of latex. The absorbent plaster will immediately begin to soak the ammonia solvent from the rubbery mixture. Let the

mold set for about fifteen minutes and pour the surplus latex back into your jar. This liquid is unharmed and can be used to make future castings.

There is a tendency for very small air bubbles to form on the surface of liquid latex. One or two (no more) squirts of very fine water mist from a spray bottle will cause the bubbles to burst immediately. Overusing the water spray, however, will dilute the latex and could ruin the casting.

Latex is very flexible—a small casting made with a single coating of latex might be strong, but a large casting, such as the turkey shown in the illustrations or a full head mask, might collapse under its own weight. It is not unusual, then, for

It is possible to rush the curing of latex with gentle heat and air motion. A hair dryer set on its lowest setting and administered from a distance of about eighteen inches is commonly used. Lay the dryer on its side and prop the mold so that the air flow is directed into the wet latex. If the latex formulation is not extremely thick, the mold should be cured in an hour or so.

the walls of a casting to be strengthened with two or more applications of latex.

You may even consider bonding a layer of fabric into the liquid rubber, as shown on the next page, to act as a reinforcement.

Reinforcing a Latex Casting with Cheesecloth

When the first coating of latex has dried, treat it as an impression coating and proceed to reinforce the thin skin with cheesecloth.

Pour about ½ cup of latex into the mold. Cut several pieces of coarse weave cheesecloth about 8″ × 12″. Lay the mold on its side and carefully place the cloth into the liquid, spreading the fabric fully open. Use a small brush to "paint" the cloth with the latex that accumulates in the bottom of the mold. Take the time required to press the cloth tightly against the dried first coating of latex. When the first piece of cloth is saturated with latex and pressed closely against the walls of the impression coating, drop a second piece in place. Treat it the same way; add each strip of cheesecloth in this manner, until the complete interior of the casting is now covered

by a criss-crossed network of fabric. If the small reservoir of liquid latex in the bottom of the mold becomes exhausted, pour in another small amount and continue till the job is finished.

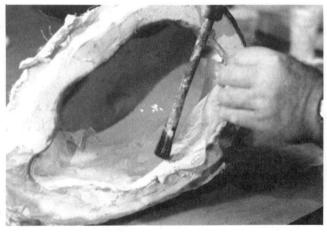

Adhere a final layer of cheesecloth around the border of the mold to thicken the bottom edge, making the edge especially strong. Most of the casting will be reinforced by at least two and possibly three overlapping layers of cheesecloth. The perimeter of the casting should have as many as four or five reinforcing layers.

Force-dry the casting with the hair dryer, or let it set undisturbed for two or three days. After the casting has dried thoroughly it can be removed from the mold.

Begin removing the casting by tugging the skin away from the mold all the way around the rim; then stick your fingers between the casting and the plaster mold to encourage further separation. Loosen the latex slowly and patiently. The deep projections of this mold need special attention. Cured latex is strong and you will be able to tug pretty hard if separation is difficult.

Neoprene Casting Rubber

Neoprene casting rubber was devised by today's polymerizing alchemists as a substitute for latex. It works a lot like the latex it was supposed to replace, but its characteristics are not the same. Neoprene cures to a much harder finish; although the casting remains flexible, it is very firm. The curing time is much less than with latex—overnight is usually sufficient.

The only practical way of making a neoprene casting is to follow the process of absorption casting. This technique involves pouring liquid neoprene into a plaster mold and allowing it to sit for a period. The solvent is absorbed into the plaster of the mold just as water is absorbed from the clay in slipcasting pottery. A thin wall is formed, and this wall remains in the mold when the excess liquid is poured out. The final casting is formed as the neoprene continues to cure, through the joint effects of evaporation and continued absorption.

No mold release is required between the plaster mold and the neoprene casting.

And while we are on the subject of mold releases, perhaps it would be wise to repeat the caution given earlier against the use of petroleum jelly on plaster molds intended for use in neoprene casting. Petroleum jelly clogs the pores of the plaster and, if used as a mold release, will most likely cause failure in the final casting. Liquid soap can be used as the release agent in the construction of the plaster mold, but it must be used sparingly.

Safety Considerations

The odors produced by neoprene are not harsh or offensive, and the fumes may seem harmless enough—but beware of overexposure. The Material Safety Data Sheet provided by the manufacturer indicates that vapors from neoprene should not be breathed. Skin contact can cause burns, and irreversible eye damage is possible if the liquid is splashed into the eyes. Skin contact must be followed by immediately flushing the skin with water. Clothing contaminated with the liquid must be removed and laundered.

SUMMARY: Use neoprene in a space where positive ventilation is provided to carry all vapors away.

The use of chemical goggles and latex gloves is recommended.

Making a Neoprene Casting

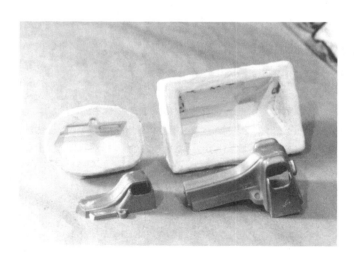

These plaster impressions were taken from authentic coffin handle supports.

The mold-making process was explained in the section on making a One-Part Plaster Mold (pages 37 to 39).

Pour the liquid neoprene into the plaster mold, filling the mold to the brim. The plaster will immediately begin to do its work on the thin liquid, absorbing the solvent from the solution. The level of the neoprene will most likely drop as the solvent is absorbed. If this happens, add more liquid neoprene in order to keep the mold filled and the rim of the casting strong.

Give the plaster plenty of time to do its work. A wait of two to three hours is required for a $^3/_{16}$″ wall to form. Less time will give you a thinner wall; more time will yield a thicker, tougher wall. Cured neoprene is a very tough, durable material. It is not likely that you would want the walls of your reproductions to be more than $^3/_{16}$″ thick.

After two to three hours, pour the unabsorbed neoprene solution back into its container for use another time. A thin skin may have formed on the surface of the liquid in the mold as a result of air drying. This contamination should be skimmed off and discarded. Almost all of the neoprene solution that was poured into the mold is recoverable.

You will find that your biggest loss will be spillage as you attempt to pour the surplus neoprene back into the jug. The stuff is so thin! The plaster mold is so unwieldy! No matter how hard you try not to, you'll end up with liquid all over the table. As you can see in the photo to the right above, our solution was to use an intermediate vessel with which we could pour the neoprene neatly back into the jug.

One further cautionary note: Airtight storage for liquid neoprene is essential. Even a very small air leak will allow the rubber to set up, and you'll find yourself with a jug of very expensive "Jello."

Wait another period of ten to twelve hours, and the castings will be ready to pull from the mold. In fact, you may find the castings to be shrinking slightly and pulling away from the sides of the plaster mold as you monitor the curing. Very gentle tugging will give you a clean separation.

Neoprene does shrink as it cures. A thin-walled casting will shrink a little; a thick-walled casting will shrink much more. This could become a matter of some concern to you if your casting must have a wall thickness over $^3/_{16}$″.

Here you can see the pattern and the mold flanked by two castings ready for trimming.

This photo illustrates the hardware in place on the corners of a coffin.

LAMINATED CASTINGS

There are an assortment of laminating materials that can be cast in a mold. The process of laminated casting involves a repeated layering of fabric or paper with some kind of binder to build up a strong wall in the finished casting. Three different laminating materials—papier-mâché,

Celastic, and fiberglass—will be demonstrated as we cast Aladdin's magic lamp.

Aladdin found his magic lamp. When you need a lamp to assist in telling his story, you'd best not expect the same good luck. You will, no doubt, be required to make your own castings.

First you will need a pattern for your mold. You could sculpt one from scratch; or you might decide, as we did, to fashion one from a teapot and mount it on a pedestal. We began with a low, squat sort of teapot that had some of the right lines and suggested possibilities for transformation into an old-fashioned oil lamp.

We added Plasticine, sculpting the pattern to make it look a little more like an oil lamp and a little less like a teapot. The addition of the pedestal to the finished casting (see page 104) will also help to convey this illusion.

This project makes use of a two-part mold. For detailed instructions, refer to the section on making a Two-Part Plaster Mold (pages 30 to 36).

The mold for this lamp was made according to the same construction technique outlined there.

Separate the pattern from the two plaster forms, and you are ready to make your reproductions.

Papier-Mâché

For years—from the time the theater came indoors until the late 1930s—the only casting materials available to theater craftsmen were plaster, clay, and papier-mâché. Some prop men in those days became artists with these materials. Techniques of using papier-mâché were developed and refined to the point that these craftsmen could build everything from paper: rosettes of paper pulp, entire sets of papier-mâché rocks, and colonnades of paper sheets supported with chicken wire forms.

Here we will examine one of several papier-mâché techniques that have been developed:

papier-mâché casting.

This technique makes use of strips of fibrous paper that have been saturated in glue. Papers with a hard or oily finish are not effective in this process; they are intended to resist moisture and water penetration, so the glue cannot soak into the fibers. Brown wrapping paper (kraft paper) makes a very strong casting; we used newspaper in the example shown. The glue you select for papier-mâché work should dry to form a hard, shell-like surface. White glue (PVA) is the most convenient binder for this use today.

Safety Considerations

You do not need to be concerned about hazards as you work with papier-mâché. Paper and white glue are both non-toxic and inoffensive. If you choose to use wallpaper paste as the binder, note that some manufacturers of wallpaper paste add poison to discourage rodents.

Mold Release

The glued paper strips will do their best to stick to a dry plaster mold, so you need to use a releasing agent between the mold and the laminations. Petroleum jelly works well for this release.

Preparing the Paper

Tear the paper into strips about 1″ × 2″. Do not *cut* the paper into strips, as this leaves a hard "cut" edge that does not blend well into the neighboring piece. For the same reason, it is a good idea to rip off the straight paper-mill edge from all around the newspaper and throw it away; just use pieces that have only torn edges.

Dip several paper strips in glue and let them soak briefly.

After the strips are saturated with glue, run one through your crossed fingers to remove some surplus paste, and press it lightly into the greased mold. Repeat the process and lay in another piece of soaked paper, overlapping its edges with the first one. Continue adding the glue-soaked strips in a criss-cross kind of patchwork, till the entire surface of the mold is covered with glued strips.

Applying the Strips

After this first application, the buildup in the mold should already be three or four layers deep due to the overlapping. When both halves of the mold are filled, go back and give each a second coating just like the first. This time, though, use the colored Sunday comic section, to make it easier to see that there are no thin spots in the second coat. Now your casting should be six or eight layers thick. Maybe the handle is filled now; that's O.K. Let the mold set and dry for a couple of hours, and then give it a final coat, this time using the editorial or classified-ad page.

Curing the Papier-Mâché

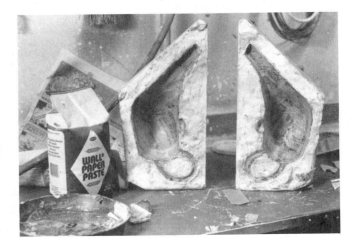

Set the castings aside and let them dry for forty-eight hours. The casting should now be dry, firm, and strong.

The casting will shrink slightly as the glue dries, and it will pull away from the walls of its mold. If this casting were attempted with a positive mold, the shrinkage would make the casting cling all the more tightly to the mold. Separation from a negative mold, therefore, is much more easily accomplished.

Finishing the Casting

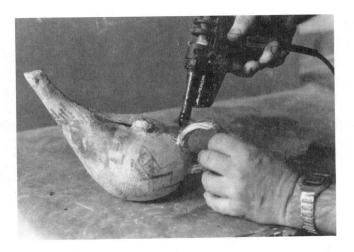

Trim the surplus material away from the edge of the casting with a pair of scissors. As you do this, make sure your scissors are snipping along a line that corresponds to the plaster line at the exact center of the casting.

Join the two halves of the lamp together with hot glue. Make every effort to have the glue penetrate deep into the joint and leave the surface of the seam flush and smooth.

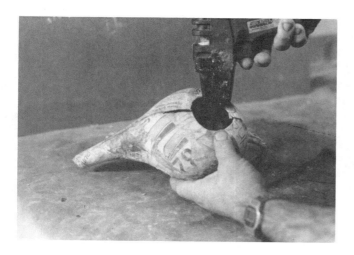

If you cut a small hole in the bottom of the lamp, you can reach inside and apply a heavier coat of glue to the inside of the seam where it will not be seen.

You can make the seam almost disappear by giving the lamp another coat of papier-mâché. The purpose of this final coating is threefold:

1. It gives the surface a harder coating.
2. It smooths out rough spots in the surface.
3. It hides the seam.

Use kraft paper this time and don't overlap the strips as much as in the earlier steps. Take particular care to spread full strips across the glued seam, and the seam will vanish.

Apply a base to the lamp, using hot glue as an adhesive. Our pedestal base was taken from a dime store-variety plastic goblet.

Celastic

Celastic is the trade name of a plastic-filled fabric which can be cast in layers very much like papier-mâché. This material, first produced commercially in the late 1940s, was one of the first "do-it-yourself" plastics to be put on the market. Theater craftsmen (especially those working in costuming and properties) saw the advantages of this new product in the construction of armor, masks, decorations, and many small construction projects where the material's high cost didn't preclude its use. The theater has been using this product for a generation now, and theater craftsmen seem to have become divided into two camps—those who consider Celastic one of the indispensable materials of the theater, and those others who (having found newer products more to their liking) regard it as passé and dispensable. I list myself with the former group, still finding many opportunities to make good use of Celastic.

Celastic is a woven material which has been treated to completely fill the fibers of the fabric with cellulose nitrate. The raw fabric is somewhat stiff but flexible (rather like pasteboard) and can be torn into strips of usable size. When soaked in the proper solvent, the cellulose nitrate dissolves, making the cloth very soft and workable. As the solvent evaporates, the cellulose nitrate cures, the stiffness returns, and the cloth holds its shape.

Safety Considerations

Acetone is a widely used solvent for Celastic, though it is a little more volatile than the once-recommended solvent methyl-ethyl-ketone, or MEK. Both solvents are extremely flammable and therefore dangerous in the presence of sparks or flames. These solvents should not be used without adequate ventilation. Acetone is harmful to lung tissue and can produce dizziness and headache. MEK is much more toxic, having been linked to permanent neurological damage; it is no longer recommended. Acetone and MEK are both irritating to the skin of most persons and should not be used without the protection of barrier lotion or rubber gloves.

I have learned to be comfortable using Celastic with my bare fingers; but I know that many people, sensitive to the effects of acetone, break out in a rash when exposed to this harsh solvent. I prefer not to use gloves of any kind because of the loss of "feedback" from the material when my sense of touch is dulled by gloves. I am convinced, however, that this is an acquired preference and not a practice that should be recommended to the beginner.

SUMMARY: Do not use Celastic solvents near a source of sparks or flames. Work in a space that is provided with forced local ventilation. Use barrier lotion or latex rubber gloves—rubber gloves are recommended.

Mold Release

After your hands have been protected with rubber gloves, the mold can be protected with a mold release. Petroleum jelly works pretty well as a release agent between Celastic and plaster. Use the petroleum jelly liberally and try to keep the first coat of Celastic from being overly saturated with solvent. Acetone can dissolve petroleum jelly, and continued massaging of the Celastic will reduce the effectiveness of the mold release.

Preparing the Celastic

Find a well-ventilated work space and fill a shallow pan with acetone. Tear up a supply of Celastic strips. For a project the size of this one, the strips can be about 1½" × 3". The strips should be torn rather than snipped with a pair of scissors. A torn edge will make a smoother "feather-edged" blend from one strip to the next than would be possible with a hard edge made by a scissor cut.

Dip a few strips of Celastic into the solvent and let them soak for a minute or so. The plastic in the weave of the cloth will soften immediately. The strips could be used without delay; but allowing them a short soak loosens the plastic filler, making it more workable. A word of caution, however: if you leave the strip in the solvent too long, the plastic will dissolve completely and float out of the fabric, leaving you with a limp piece of rag.

Applying the Celastic Laminations

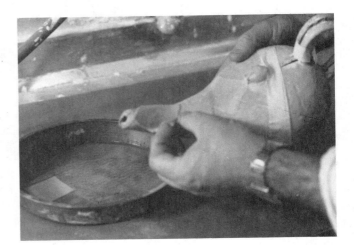

Lay the first strip into your mold. Grab another wetted strip, run it between your fingers to wring out any extra solvent, and overlap it on one edge of the first strip. Create a criss-cross pattern of strips inside the mold. Massage the overlapped strips with your finger, working the plastic filler into the fabric till the strips are blended smoothly together.

Continue in this manner until both halves of the mold are covered with criss-crossing layers of wetted plastic strips. The handles will probably turn out to be solidly filled with Celastic strips. Incidentally, the strips which extend into the handle should start well into the body of the lamp, thereby eliminating the possibility of a weak spot where the handle joins the body.

Curing the Castings

Let the filled mold halves rest overnight. The solvent will evaporate, leaving a thin, strong, hard shell.

Next day, pull the Celastic castings out of the molds. They should be hard and dry. If they are dry or almost dry, you can begin to trim the edges. If, on the other hand, the castings are still damp and even the least bit flimsy, put them back into the molds, give them some more time —and be patient.

Using the plaster mold as a guide, draw a pen line on the Celastic casting. This marking is to indicate where the two halves will join. Cut the surplus material away with a sharp mat knife or a pair of tin snips.

Use masking tape to fasten the halves together temporarily, and begin to cover the seam with a coating of Celastic strips. This application of Celastic need not cover the entire lamp, just the seam where the halves connect. Don't be too concerned that this coat will change the shape or proportions of the lamp design. Celastic is very thin and one layer will not significantly increase the lamp's girth.

As each strip of Celastic is applied to the seam, "polish" its edges with a flat tool. (Actually, anytime you work on the exterior surface of an object—one that will be seen in the finished product—you should treat it by pressing the soft plastic around the perimeter of each Celastic strip very flat, feather-edging it with the flat edge of a knife blade or some other appropriate flattening tool. A great deal of later sanding can be eliminated with just a little of this kind of attention now.)

When the seam is dry enough to have some strength (thirty minutes or so), remove the masking tape and work on the area that the tape had concealed. The casting can now be puttied (fur-

ther reducing the amount of sanding that will be needed later) by rubbing it with an application of liquefied nitrocellulose obtained from a wad of supersaturated Celastic. Soak a strip of Celastic in acetone till the nitrocellulose is nearly dissolved and hanging on to the fabric only as a result of being trapped in the weave of the cloth (two to three minutes). Use this wad of drastically softened plastic to rub the rough spots on the exterior surface of the casting. You will find that this rubbing transfers the plastic from the cloth and leaves it in the surface depressions, bridging over any raw edges made by the patchwork of Celastic strips. Discard the wad of Celastic when the dissolved plastic has been exhausted.

Finishing the Castings

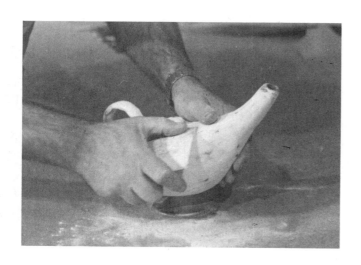

Give the seam reinforcement overnight to dry, and then sand the entire lamp to blend the edges of any strips that are still asserting their individual identities.

Give the lamp a coating of primer and, if necessary, apply a thin coat of spackle to help blend the edges, seams, and overlaps.

Sand the spackle, spray the lamp with another coating of primer, and sand it again. Attach the stand before giving the lamp its "finish" coat of paint.

Fiberglass

Fiberglass is just what its name implies—real glass, spun into a fiber. The fiber, as fine as a strand of a spider's web, is made into threads and then woven into cloth. This cloth has the texture and some of the qualities of textile fabric; it also has some of the characteristics of glass.

Have you ever thought about how hard it is to destroy glass? You would have to shatter it and then grind it up. Glass is flameproof; it is extremely resistant to the effects of age and sunlight; and it cannot decay. Fiberglass has the same positive qualities.

Polyester resin, when it cures, becomes very dry and brittle. It is a little surprising that when you mix this brittle plastic into the flexible glass cloth, it cures into a product with unbelievable strength. Its strength-to-weight ratio is in a class by itself. Fiberglass is so strong that boats and automobile bodies can be made from it—and these bodies are much lighter than if they had been made of metal.

In the mid 1950s fiberglass and polyester resin became available to the theater community. But the use of fiberglass did not instantly and universally capture the hearts of theater technicians as Celastic had. There were several reasons for hesitance in accepting this new plastic material. It was dangerous in several ways, and the manufacturers tended to be (at least in those early days) discouraging to the small-time user. The manu-facturers I talked to in Los Angeles in the early 1960s were much more eager to protect themselves with disclaimers concerning their product than to make helpful suggestions as to its proper use. They were willing only to provide the raw materials, with appropriate warnings; the user could experiment at his own risk. This lack of confidence on the part of the manufacturers had a chilling effect on the enthusiasm of most of those potential users who made inquiries.

With the passage of time many of the dangers of the products have been eliminated, and quality control is now assured. Several formulations of resin are now available for specific applications; if you follow the instructions provided by the manufacturer, every attempt to use today's fiberglass products should prove successful.

The techniques of working with papier-mâché, Celastic, and fiberglass are so similar that one begins to fantasize a sort of family relationship among them. In fact there is no comparison in the quality of the finished products; but most of the techniques appropriate to papier-mâché and Celastic can be carried over to casting with fiberglass. While you must use a brush to control the resin and apply the fiberglass, never using your fingers (even gloved) to work with these materials, you will find that most other techniques carry over.

Safety Considerations

Polyester resin, a necessary component in the fiberglass process, is one of the more dangerous materials you can use in casting, and it must be used with all caution. Improper use of fiberglass chemicals can cause dermatitis, nasal irritation, dizziness, weakness, nausea, headache, blurred vision, and almost every ill you can imagine except cancer (it seems this hazard has been designed out of the product). The resin contains a styrene compound which is highly toxic by inhalation or ingestion, moderately toxic through skin contact, and flammable. The catalyst used to cure the resin, methyl-ethyl-ketone peroxide (MEK peroxide), is pretty powerful stuff—caustic and corrosive to all parts of the human machinery. The body part that is most likely to be exposed to this chemical's ill effects is the skin of your arms and hands. Most susceptible to damage is eye tissue. If this chemical is splashed in your eyes, the damage can be permanent.

MEK peroxide is the recommended catalyst for polyester resin; acetone is the recommended cleanup solvent. It is likely, therefore, that you will be using both of these chemicals in the same working space. You should be aware that if you mix undiluted MEK peroxide with acetone, the mixture can explode. Don't let this intimidate you unduly, but do respect it and be careful.

Use polyester resin in a well-ventilated area. The fumes are hard on the linings of your lungs, and they can contaminate foodstuffs. The vapors from uncured resins are flammable. There should be no smoking in the area in which you are working — not only because of the fire danger, but also because of the possible transfer of chemicals from your hands to the cigarette and from the cigarette to your mouth.

It is generally known that if a little extra catalyst is mixed into polyester resin, the resin sets up faster. This acceleration is accompanied by the emission of heat, which you may be able to detect by touching the casting. In some cases adding extra catalyst is a recommended procedure. How-

ever, if you add an excessive amount, the heat released will also be excessive. If you use too much catalyst, the casting will discolor and crack or, at worst, it will burst into flames. Don't be intimidated; just be careful — you are in control of the amount of catalyst used. If the instructions call for twenty drops, don't use a tablespoonful.

SUMMARY: Do not breathe the fumes of uncured polyester resin. Work in a space that is supplied with forced ventilation, and wear an approved vapor respirator. Wear goggles when mixing MEK peroxide. Wear latex gloves when working with the catalyst or liquid resin. Mix the catalyst according to the manufacturer's directions. Do not work in the presence of sparks or flames.

It may seem that there are a lot of safety rules associated with polyester resins. This is because polyester resins are one of the most dangerous casting materials discussed in this book.

Mold Release

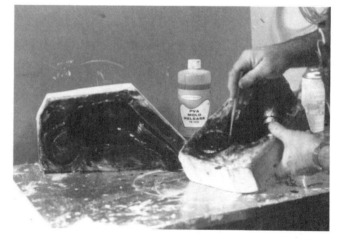

When you cast with fiberglass and polyester resin, you must put special care into the preparation of the mold. The plaster mold must be sealed in a way that will not result in the coats of mold release being absorbed by the plaster. The petroleum jelly that was recommended for use with Celastic castings does not work well with fiberglass. Petroleum jelly tends to inhibit the surface cure of the resin where the resin is in contact with the mold.

A coat of paint applied to the plaster will act as a sealant. After the paint has dried, the mold

is ready to be treated with mold release. Experts who work with polyester resins daily recommend polyvinyl alcohol (PVA) for this purpose. PVA may be applied directly with a brush or sprayed with an airbrush. As you apply this liquid, you are covering the sealed plaster with a thin coating of vinyl, one of those plastics that almost nothing will adhere to. The solvent in PVA is alcohol, which evaporates quickly; drying can even be rushed by force-heating it with a hair dryer. A second coat of PVA makes the vinyl coating thicker.

Making an Impression Coat

Before making the impression coating, prepare your hands by putting on gloves or applying a barrier cream. Use an inexpensive brush or a tool of some kind in each step of the operation; make every effort to keep the resin from touching your hands.

Pour about two ounces of laminating resin into a clean container.

Following the instructions provided by the manufacturer of the product you are using, add the proper amount of catalyst. The product we are using in the photos calls for twenty drops to make a controlled "hot" mixture that will set up quickly.

Stir the mixture carefully and thoroughly.

Paint a coating of this "hot" catalyzed resin onto the entire surface of the mold as an impression coating. Any air bubbles that might later get caught in the fiberglass casting will not come through this smooth impression coating to spoil the casting.

Special-purpose polyester resins have been formulated. There is a resin called "gel coat" designed specifically for use in making impression coatings. It is thicker than other resins and clings better to the sides of the mold. You can save yourself a lot of frustration by using gel coat for the impression coating, if you can obtain some. Otherwise, just keep brushing the resin out of the puddles and back onto the walls of the mold till it begins to set up.

Applying the Fiberglass

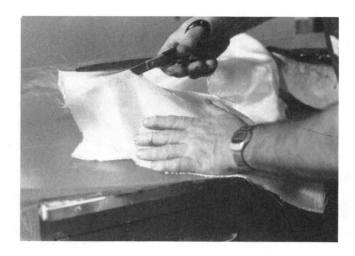

Laminating the fiberglass requires a fiberglass cloth of medium weight. Select such a cloth and cut it into strips about 2″ × 4″. The loose weave of the cloth allows some freedom of movement. The cloth won't stretch, but it will conform to some of the irregularities of a rounded surface.

Lay a strip of fiberglass cloth into the mold and coat it with an application of catalyzed resin. Lay in another piece of cloth partly overlapping the first one, and dab at it with the brush. The second strip of cloth will soak up some of the surplus resin from the first patch.

Add more resin as is necessary to wet the cloth completely. Continue in this manner till the molding surface is entirely covered with overlapping strips of fiberglass cloth.

You can tell when you have used enough resin: the cloth will lose its white color and become almost transparent. It is, of course, possible to use too much resin. This would make the casting thicker and heavier without adding significantly to its strength.

Be alert for air bubbles that might form between the glass cloth and the wall of the mold. Use your brush to push the cloth back in place, thereby eliminating any air pockets and potential flaws in the casting.

For an object the size of our magic lamp, two applications of criss-crossed fiberglass strips should be enough. Making the walls of the cast-

ing thicker with more coatings of fiberglass *will* make the unit stronger—but how strong does this lamp have to be?

Immediately clean your brush and work area with acetone. Once the resin sets, no solvent will be useful in removing it. Your skin should not have been in contact with the resin and therefore should need no clean-up. If you have not been careful and have come in contact with the solution, remove the resin from your hands with acetone and then scrub your hands thoroughly with soap and water.

Once the molds are filled, set them aside to cure. In a couple of hours the castings should show signs of getting warm; they should also have firmed up enough to hold their shape, and yet be "green" enough to be somewhat flexible. I recommend that the castings be pulled from the molds at this stage of curing. If you wait till the castings have cured fully, they will have become very hard and stiff, making it nearly impossible for you to separate hard castings from hard molds. So break the seal that exists between the mold and the casting at this point, and then replace the casting so it will not warp as the curing continues. Once this seal has been broken, you should have no difficulty removing the cured casting later, unless the mold has extreme undercuts.

Uniting the Halves

The plaster molds can be fitted together to make a complete lamp. It follows, then, that if you mark and cut the castings right along the edge of the plaster mold, the two fiberglass castings will also fit together perfectly. Use a felt-tip marker to draw a line on the casting that corresponds to the edge of the mold. Cut away all of the surplus fiberglass overhanging the edge of the mold by trimming along this line.

If the casting is only one or two layers thick, and if it is still a little bit "green," you should be able to do this trimming with a pair of scissors. If, however, the casting is too thick or too hard, you may have to resort to a band saw or a hacksaw to make the cut.

Test the fit of the halves of the casting, and if they don't meet as perfectly as they should, trim them until they do. Hold the castings in alignment with a wrap or two of masking tape until the union is made secure with a carefully applied coat of fiberglass and resin.

Prepare for the job of sealing the seam between the two castings by cutting some fiberglass cloth into strips about 1″ × 3″. Suit up with your safety equipment; then pour a small amount of resin into a small cup and add the proper amount of catalyst (according to label instructions on the product you are using). Stir the mixture till the ingredients are thoroughly combined.

Lay one of the strips of fiberglass cloth across the seam, and brush a coat of resin into the threads of the cloth. Make this application as smooth as possible, and try to confine the application to the area immediately adjacent to the joint. Continue applying fiberglass and resin along the seam till the crack between the two halves is sealed.

Finishing the Casting

Casting resin separates from a glass mold with a surface as smooth as the glass itself. However, laminating resin cast in a plaster mold must be sanded and filled in order to have the same glassy finish. This is especially true where two halves of a casting have been joined with a surface application of fiberglass as we have done with our lamp. The surface *can* be made as smooth as glass, but

it will take a lot of sanding and putty and paint to do it.

Plastic body filler is a very good putty to use in filling surface imperfections on a polyester resin and fiberglass casting. See the section on Plastic Body Filler (pages 165 to 168) for complete instructions on the use of this polyester-based product.

Safety Considerations

In all stages of fiberglass finishing, be very aware of the danger posed by the dust. Fiberglass dust contains not only irritating and poisonous chemicals, but also microscopic particles of glass which, *once inside your lungs, will become lifelong and potentially deadly companions.*

SUMMARY: Wear a particle mask when filing or sanding fiberglass castings.

Using a rasp, file the roughest portions of the lamp. You don't need to file the whole lamp; just go over the roughest spots where you patched the seam. If you made the join carefully, the rest of the lamp will still be too smooth to attack with a tool as coarse as a rasp.

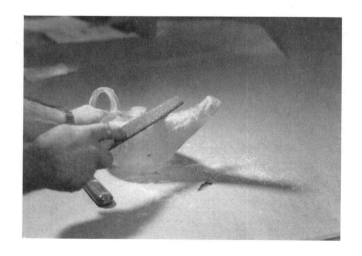

Apply body filler with a putty knife or small rubber squeegee. Make this application as smooth as possible, but don't be distressed by a little roughness. This material is designed to be easily sanded.

When the putty starts to become firm—in half an hour or so—it is ready to work. While the putty is in this semi-cured "butter" stage, a wood rasp or Sur-form (trade name for a file designed specifically for putty and foam) can be used to easily remove the rough places. As the putty gets progressively harder, of course, the roughness will become harder to remove.

As you continue working on the lamp with the file, the putty will continue to harden. When you have done all you can with the file, the lamp will probably be ready for sanding.

Sanding an object such as our lamp should be done in two or three stages. First, a coarse-grit sandpaper (#60 or #80) is used to smooth out the file marks. Second, the scratches from the coarse sandpaper should be smoothed out with a #100 or #150 grit sandpaper. If you want a glass-smooth finish like that on a fine auto paint job, go on to the third stage: paint the lamp with a primer, and sand the primer smooth with #320 grit.

Our lamp was finished with a coat of gold paint.

HOT MELTS AND THERMOPLASTICS

A hot melt is solid at room temperature; it liquefies and is moldable when it is heated. Many hotmelt products are relatively new, but some of them have been in use for years. The materials in this classification that have long been useful to the property builder are: wax, moulage (already discussed in the section on The Mold, pages 48 to 50), wax-based modeling clay, and hot-melt rubber. More recently introduced thermoplastics include polyvinyl chloride (PVC), acrylic, styrene, and polyolefin (polyethylene vinyl acetate), the stuff that hot-melt glue is made of.

Most hot melts can be recycled. You can reclaim one of these products if you are careful to not contaminate it with foreign matter.

Safety Considerations

There are a few major hazards common to hot-melt casting materials.

There is a constant hazard when working with molten materials that you might be burnt by accidental spills. Wearing protective clothing can minimize this problem. Some flammable materials are advertised as being useful for making prosthetic molds directly from human skin, but you can be badly burned from improperly making this kind of casting. Wax and moulage can be used directly on the skin, but the heated materials must be allowed to cool below 140°F. in order for your skin to tolerate the heat. Thrusting your hand into molten wax or moulage will cause severe burns.

If a flammable material is heated beyond its flash point, it is reasonable to expect it to burst into flames. This danger can be avoided by heating with a double boiler or electric oven whenever practical, and by using a thermometer to monitor the actual temperature of the molten material.

Keep a fire extinguisher within reach, and know how to use it. CO_2 and dry powder extinguishers are effective when you are working with hot melts. You should not need any fire-fighting equipment, but it is important to know where the extinguisher is when you do need it.

Overheating some of the thermoplastics will cause smoke, and in almost all cases the smoke produced will be toxic.

SUMMARY: Wear protective clothing — leather gloves, leather apron, goggles — to guard against spills of molten material. Use a double boiler or electric oven when practical. Monitor the actual temperature of the heated material, and do not exceed the recommended melting temperature. If you are working with one of the thermoplastics capable of producing toxic smoke, work only in a space provided with forced-air ventilation.

These cautions are introductory and general. Further precautions will be noted as we discuss specific materials.

Wax (Paraffin)

You are probably familiar with wax as a casting material. The figures in nineteenth-century wax museums were, of course, made of wax. Psychics used wax impressions of hands to dupe clients in seances early in this century. Sherlock Holmes once aided his detective work by making a wax impression of a key. Molds for metal castings (bronze, aluminum, gold) are still made by a process involving "lost wax."

Today's doll makers have added a hardener to the wax they use, and they may cast their wax in silicone molds; but the techniques of using the material have not changed much over the years.

Candle makers have formulated a wide variety of waxes. Some are very soft; these usually burn rapidly and create a profusion of drippings that decorate the candle and its holder. Others are hard, burning very slowly with low light output and almost no drippings. It is this harder wax that will be of greater interest to us as a prop-building material.

Paraffin wax will mix with certain polyester additives (available from hobby shops that handle candle-making supplies) that increase the hardness of the wax. The ratio of plastic to wax can be increased till the mixture is almost entirely plastic; however, the polyester beads that are used as wax hardeners are themselves rather soft. There is an optimum proportion of hardener that will effectively increase the hardness of the wax; if the object you are making needs to be very hard and durable, it is probably best to select another casting material.

The product shown in the next few illustrations is the hardest grade of wax available over the counter. It was intended for use in making dripless candles; we will be using it to make a pair of puppet feet.

Heating the Wax

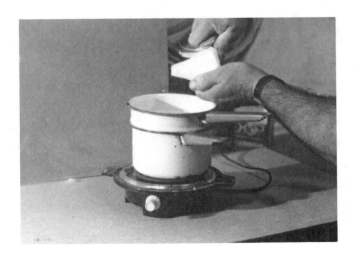

Use a paring knife to reduce the cake of wax to small slivers. Heat these slivers in a double boiler. This operation may remind you of one you have witnessed in your childhood—your mother or grandmother heating paraffin to seal the jars when she made jelly.

Do not melt wax by applying heat directly. Using a double boiler helps to control overheating and minimizes the danger of flash fire.

Stir the wax with a spoon or clean stick. The wax will melt at about 160°F., and it will probably be melted by the time the water is boiling.

When a hot casting material is poured slowly into a cold mold, a flaw called a *freeze line* may form. Freeze lines are caused when a cold mold cools the melted casting material and prevents it from blending smoothly with the subsequent flow.

Freeze lines can be prevented by preheating the mold to about 110°F. in an electric oven and then pouring in the casting material quickly in one continuous motion.

Pouring the Mold

Pour the hot wax directly into a silicone mold. Wait for two or three hours for the wax to cool and harden. The plaster-encased silicone mold will hold heat for a long time, so don't become impatient and open the mold prematurely.

Wax shrinks a little as it cools, so it's a good idea to monitor the casting and top it off with little extra pourings of wax if they are needed.

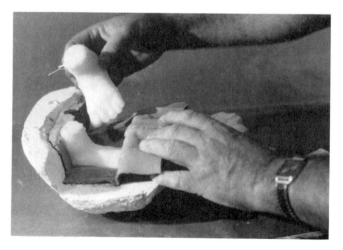

The finished casting should release from the silicone mold with a minimum of effort.

Machinable Wax

There is a wax on the market with a hardness comparable to soft aluminum. Called *machinable wax*, it is manufactured for use in machine shops to test the accuracy of milling and drilling setups.

Machinable wax melts, pours, and sets up just like candle wax. Since it sets up so hard, its uses in making molds and castings are obvious.

This wax melts at about 250°F. and its flash point is very high—about 575°F. The danger of fire with machinable wax is far less than with candle wax, but there is an increased danger of severe burns resulting from accidental spillage.

A paring knife won't make a dent in this wax; you'll have to use a band saw to cut pieces of a workable size from the block of wax.

You will get nowhere trying to melt this wax in a double boiler—since its melting point is higher than water's boiling point, machinable wax cannot be made hot enough to melt in a water boiler. Direct heat on a single-level pan works fine, but some caution is necessary to avoid fire. Do not leave the pot unattended, and as soon as the wax is melted it should be removed from the heat and poured into your mold.

Silicone is a good material to use for your mold when you are making a hot-melt casting. The construction of this mold for a cane handle was detailed earlier in the section on silicone mold making.

After you have poured the wax into the mold, let the poured casting set for two to three hours, and it will be ready to open. This wax is capable of very high quality reproduction. Its only drawback, as far as I know, is that it is brittle and therefore susceptible to breakage.

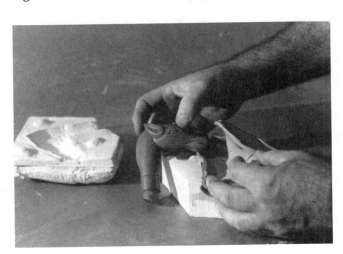

Hot Plasticine

Non-drying modeling clay is available in two forms—oil-based and wax-based. Oil-based clay breaks down when it is heated into oil and unmoldable solids. The wax-based clay, however, retains its identity when it is heated. Since it is a progeny of wax, it will perform in a manner very much like its parent: it can be melted in a double boiler and poured into a mold, and when it is cooled, it will turn into a solid that appears to be a clay sculpture of the pattern used to make the mold.

The following process is one you will find useful when you need a clay copy of an object.

Making a Soft Pattern

There are times when you will have a "hard" pattern—one made of, say, porcelain—and you realize that you would be far better off with a "soft" pattern, one that you could use to make a plaster mold. After all, the most successful "hard" mold is obtained from a flexible pattern. (This is a fact you're bound to have caught on to by now, if you've read this book up to here.)

A two-step process is required in order to construct a good quality "soft" pattern from the "hard" pattern you have to begin with. First, a negative mold must be made; from this mold, a positive clay figure can be cast using melted modeling clay.

Making the Negative Mold

The first impression—the negative mold—could be made of alginate. This material is both flexible and capable of high-fidelity reproduction of detail. (Review Prosthetics, page 43, for a detailed explanation of the use of alginate.)

Mix the alginate, and pour the paste over your pattern. As soon as the alginate has set and you have removed the surplus congealed material from your hands, split the mold up the back and remove the pattern.

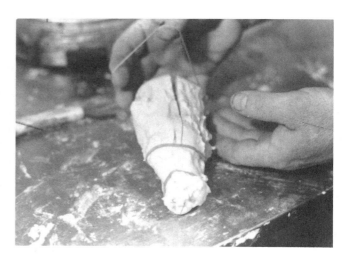

Gently wiggle the pattern within the mold, lift the flaps of the split alginate, and free the pattern by allowing it to slide from its alginate glove. A mold for a figure as small as the one shown will hold its own shape; a larger object will most likely require a plaster mother mold.

The break in the alginate mold can be secured with a restraint consisting of rubber bands. For an object of this size, four or five rubber bands should be sufficient. Exact alignment of the split will not be possible, and a visible seamline up the back of the positive casting will be the result.

Mold Release

No mold release is necessary to separate wax-based modeling clay from alginate.

Making the Casting

Slice off a chunk of modeling clay that you judge to be about the right quantity. (It's better to prepare a little too much than to run short.) Use new, uncontaminated clay for this process. Cut the chunk into small pieces and put them in a double boiler. The clay will melt when the water in the lower pan begins to boil. Wax-based clay melts at about 180°F., and it will discolor if it is exposed to too much direct heat.

Keep a constant watch on your pot. As soon as the clay has melted, pour it into the alginate mold. Pour the hot Plasticine in a continuous stream, keeping a steady hand. If there is any interruption or hesitation in your pouring, a "freeze line" will most likely be formed where the arrested flow of clay was cooled by the moist alginate; subsequent pouring cannot blend perfectly with the cooled portion.

The clay will cool completely in about an hour. As soon as it does, you can open the mold and remove your "soft pattern."

A two-part plaster mold can now be made from the soft clay pattern. Treat the soft pattern the same as you would a hard pattern.

Hot clay will soon dry the moisture from an alginate mold, but you should be able to make at least two copies of your original before the mold's short life expires.

When the plaster has set, the clay pattern can be removed from the mold. Since this pattern is flexible, it can be pried loose even if it contains undercuts. You might spoil the clay model, but you now have a good "hard" casting of your pattern.

Reproductions may be made from this plaster mold using any of the materials demonstrated in the section on laminated castings, from your choice of one of the flexible materials, or from one of the materials that utilizes the absorption process.

Hot Melt Glue

Hot-melt glue (ethylene vinyl acetate or EVA) is a thermoplastic with qualities much like those of other hot melts: it becomes fluid when heated, and is ruggedly solid when it cools to room tem-perature. In fact, it has enough of the "right" characteristics to make it a useful casting material. We will demonstrate casting with hot glue as we construct a crown from scratch.

The filigree headband of this crown was made of a standard lamp part, called "brass banding." The finials are twenty repeated castings of EVA (hot-melt glue).

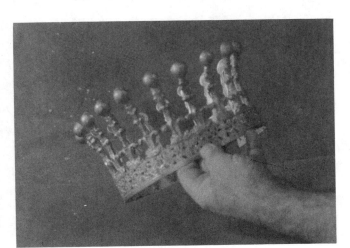

Making the Pattern

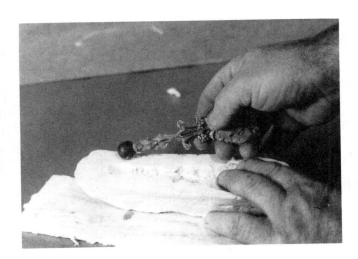

If you are good at sculpting, you might want to model your own pattern for the finial using a hard grade of Plasticine. However, we made ours from an ornamental piece of metal intended to decorate a bureau drawer. Some of the weak deli-cate joints had to be reinforced with clay. The shallow relief was built up in some places in order to accentuate the lines. We capped off the spire with half of the most regal-looking wooden bead we could find.

Making the Plaster Mold

Lay your pattern on a solid surface and apply liquid soap or petroleum jelly as a mold release.

Make a mold of the pattern as explained in the section on one-piece mold making: mix up some plaster; make an impression coating; con-

tinue adding plaster to a depth of one inch.

When the heat caused by the curing of the plaster has cooled (about two hours), you can remove the pattern from the plaster casting.

Mold Release

Hot glue will not stick to a moist surface, so water can be used as a releasing agent. Submerge the mold momentarily in a bowl of water. One dip-

ping should be enough to release two or three hot-glue castings.

Making the Hot Glue Castings

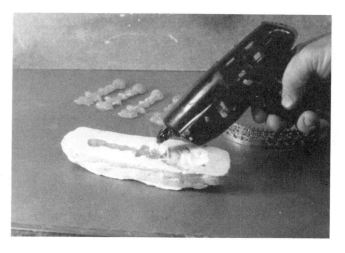

Use a hot-glue gun to squirt hot glue into the mold till the mold is filled to its brim. Bubbles are likely to form as the hot glue touches the wet plaster and turns some of the plaster's moisture to steam. These bubbles are only mildly troublesome — they can be displaced by pressing on the casting as it begins to cool but while it is still soft. *Do not touch the hot glue while it is in the liquid state, as severe burns can result.*

It takes about five minutes for the glue to cool sufficiently for it to be removed from the mold. In a couple of hours you should have the twenty castings needed to complete the crown.

It will take a full four-inch stick of hot-melt glue to make each finial the size of those shown. If the glue sticks cost twenty cents apiece, this crown will cost you about four dollars in hot glue.

Trimming and Finishing

Surplus glue must be removed from the castings. This flashing can be removed with the sharp blade of a mat knife.

Add a piece of coat hanger wire to the back side of each spire so it will hold a slight curve. Hot glue can be used to hold the wire in place. Hot glue can also be used to secure the finials around the rim of the crown.

Spray the crown with gold paint. "Jewels" could be hot-glued to the headband or to the finial tips, and a puffed lining of red or purple velvet might also be added.

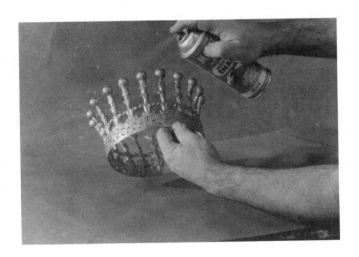

Hot-Melt Rubber

Hot-melt rubber, compounded from polyvinyl chloride (PVC), will melt when it is heated to about 350°F. When cooled, it takes on the shape of the form it was poured around or into. Castings made of hot-melt rubber are solid but very soft, flexible, tough, and resilient. This product can also be formed over a pattern, producing a successful mold in a very short time. The reproductive capabilities of hot-melt rubber do not compare favorably with those of silicone RTV, but for most applications hot-melt rubber is good enough, and since there is no curing time involved, speed is an advantage. The product is packaged by several manufacturers, but all versions work in about the same way. The rubber comes in shreds or chunks and can be heated in an electric oven or a double boiler.

Safety Considerations

The high temperature required to liquefy hot-melt rubber is itself a hazard. You must always be very careful to prevent accidental spills.

The danger of fire, discussed at the beginning of the section on hot-melt casting, is especially acute when hot-melt rubber is heated with a double boiler. The greatest danger occurs when the top pan is removed from the heat so that the rubber may be poured. At that time the heavy fumes from the heated oil will roll out of the bottom pan and fall onto the heating element of the hot plate. Use of the wrong kind of oil could cause the fumes to ignite at that moment. It is important that the whole double boiler be taken well away from the heat source before the top pan is removed so that you may pour the molten rubber into your mold.

Hot-melt polyvinyl chloride gives off vinyl chloride fumes if it is overheated — these are both poisonous and carcinogenic.

SUMMARY: Work in a space that is ventilated with forced air. Monitor the material as it heats; do not allow it to overheat to the smoking and charring stage. Use a vapor respirator, and wear leather gloves and a leather apron. Have a fire extinguisher handy and know how to use it.

Hot-melt rubber cannot be melted in a pan over direct heat. Direct heat will burn the rubber on the bottom of the pan. This not only releases dangerous vinyl chloride fumes; it also creates a burnt crust that will contaminate the rest of the rubber, act as a heat insulator, and prevent the rubber in the top of the pan from receiving sufficient heat to melt.

Heating the Hot Melt Rubber

An electric turkey roaster (with a temperature control in good working order) is excellent for heating hot-melt rubber to its melting point. If you choose to use an electric oven of this sort for melting or force-drying plastic materials, the oven should be dedicated to this purpose and never again be used for preparing food. An oven in your kitchen at home should never be used for molding and casting projects because of the danger of contamination.

In order to reach the required 350°F. in a double boiler, you must use a high-temperature oil in the bottom pan of the boiler. Water turns to steam at 212°F., and therefore can never get hot enough to melt the rubbery material. Castor oil or a 50-wt. motor oil which has a high flash point can be used as the heating agent.

Fill the lower pan of your double boiler about one-third full with castor oil or a motor oil that has a high flash point (Golden Shell #40 or equivalent).

Drop the shredded rubber into the top pan of the double boiler.

As the oil begins to heat up, it will transfer heat uniformly to all parts of the upper pan, and the rubber will become a liquid.

Put a lid on the double boiler to conserve the heat. Stir the mixture occasionally till the rubber has become a thick liquid. No matter how long this takes, *do not leave the pot unattended.*

Pouring the Casting

When the rubber is pourable, remove the double boiler a safe distance from the heat source, sepa-

rate the top pan, and pour the rubber into your mold. If you use a plaster mold, do not use one that has been freshly made. If the plaster is fresh, the molten rubber will cause steam to be released from the plaster, resulting in air bubbles in the casting. It takes about *two weeks* for the excess moisture trapped in the crystals of fresh plaster to dry sufficiently.

This photo shows the rubber being poured into the fish mold whose construction was explained in detail in Two-Part Plaster Mold (pages 30 to 36).

No mold release is necessary with this product. Hot melt rubber will not stick to anything and is self-releasing.

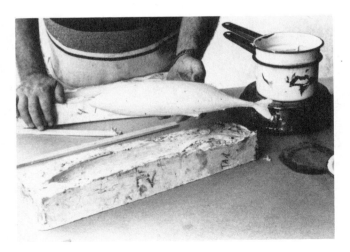

A large mold may take as long as an hour to cool. A thick plaster mold acts as an insulator, and it takes a long time for it to lose its heat.

When it is cool, the rubber casting should separate easily from the mold.

Painting a PVC Casting

The casting can be painted...but first apply a "primer" coat of spray adhesive to the entire casting. Conventional paints will not stick well to hot-melt rubber, but they will stick to a coating of spray adhesive. The fish received a base coat of gray acrylic scene paint; the underbelly was sprayed with silver and light blue from aerosol cans (an airbrush would have worked too). The eyes and fins were touched up with black. Hot-melt rubber made the tail section convincingly flexible and strong.

Cleanup

Hot-melt rubber will not stick to the pan. Truly trouble-free cleanup is a great advantage of this material.

The rubber left over from this project can be recycled. If it is not contaminated, the congealed rubber in the pan can be cut into chunks and reused as if it were fresh product. Obsolete molds and castings may also be re-melted and reused if they are clean.

BREAKAWAY GLASS

Sugar Glass

Some years ago, somebody must have taken a close look at a broken lollipop and noticed that it was transparent, strong, and brittle, and that the shards were dull enough to not be dangerous. He must have reasoned that if only he could make the lollipop large enough—the size of a window-pane, say—that an actor could fall through it without getting hurt. The notion of a window-sized all-day sucker might have been amusing at first, but somebody tried it, and it worked.

Let the pot continue at a gentle boil, unstirred, till it reaches 300°F. This temperature will be reached when nearly all of the water has been boiled away. It was 3:20 when our mixture had

The procedure for making sugar glass is included here more for historical interest than practical use, since the introduction of resins suitable for making breakaway glass (see next page) have made sugar glass obsolete.

Sugar-glass technology is a very inexact science. The shelf life of the glass is short; the castings are affected by both gravity and humidity. Left stored for even a few days, they warp and sag, become tacky, and attract ants.

The recipe for making sugar glass calls for:
    2 cups water
    1 cup white corn syrup
    3½ cups sugar
    ¼ teaspoon cream of tartar

Mix the ingredients thoroughly. Set the pan on a hot plate and let the mixture come to a boil. We started this batch at 2:30; it began to boil at 2:45. A candy thermometer will show the temperature of the boiling liquid to be about 220°F.

cooked to this point. The temperature rose very slowly to about 250°F; then it began to rise more rapidly, increasing at the rate of about 5° per minute during the last ten minutes.

When the mixture reaches 300°F. it is ready to be poured immediately.

This bottle and windowpane were made of sugar glass.

Picco Resin Breakaway Glass

The quality and reliability of breakaway windows improved dramatically when picco resins were made available. Picco resins are easy to use; even if you are inexperienced, success can be assured if you follow the simple rules outlined here. A small shop can also produce breakaway bottles using a silicone mold.

Let's make the windowpane first.

Make a Masonite or plywood pattern cut to the pane's intended dimensions. It is easier to make a mullioned window with four small panes than a single large pane. You can handle small panes with less fear of their breaking prematurely. The project illustrated is for a window 11″ × 14″.

Prepare four lengths of heavy strap iron or angle iron by adding a strip of Teflon tape to one edge of each piece. These metal strips will serve as retaining walls as you mold the pane, and the Teflon will ensure easy removal after the pane has cooled. If you don't have Teflon tape, you might be able to get along without it. Picco resins do not adhere tightly to iron and you will probably be able to remove the jigs without causing enough stress to break the pane . . . but each compromise increases the likelihood of failure.

A commercial special effects shop will have its glass-making room sealed to prevent drafts in the work space. Doors will be weatherstripped to block air currents, and the presence of visitor traffic during the pouring and cooling stages of the glass-making process will be discouraged. It is not essential that you go to such extreme measures when you cast breakaways, but you should be aware of drafts of cool air and do what you can to eliminate them.

A fully-equipped shop will have a large table specially designed for pouring window panes. The table might be as large as 4′ × 6′ (or even larger) and have a metal slab top. This metal table top will have gas jets beneath it with which it can be preheated to about 175°F. Preheating controls the rate at which the poured resin loses its heat, forcing it to cool slowly. This eliminates breakage that might be caused by the stress of fast, uneven cooling.

We are producing a small pane of glass, so a large table is not necessary. To substitute for the metal table top, we'll be using a thick sheet of stainless steel, which we'll heat in the oven from our vacuum forming machine. It is important that the steel plate be thick so it does not warp when it is heated.

If you do not have the facilities to preheat a thick sheet of metal, you might be able to get away with not using one. Premature breakage of the windowpane is possible, however, if cooling is not controlled somewhat.

Lay a sheet of cellophane or polyethylene over the preheated "table." This sheet of plastic will peel from the window pane when the casting has cooled, leaving a high gloss on the surface from which it was removed.

Arrange the prepared angle iron retainers around the plywood or Masonite pattern.

Then carefully remove the pattern without disturbing the metal frame. The mold is now ready to receive the liquid resin.

Safety Considerations

The materials used to make breakaway glass must be heated to very high temperatures. Sugar glass must reach 300°F. in order to crystallize, and picco resins must attain 400°F. to melt sufficiently for pouring. Proper protective clothing must be worn by everyone in the work area when materials are heated to such high temperatures. Common sense demands that you wear leather gloves, leather apron, and a clear face shield to protect you from accidents with these potentially disabling hot liquids.

Heating the Resins

There are two picco resins that go into the boiling pot to make up your casting mixture. The manufacturer recommends a half-and-half mix of Picco-tex 120 and Picco-lastic 125. I have found that various prop shops have their own variations on this recipe; some use a ratio of as much as two parts Picco-lastic to each part of Picco-tex. We use the recommended one-to-one ratio.

Mix the Picco-tex 120 and Picco-lastic 125 in a clean metal pot and heat the resins to 400°F. Use a candy thermometer to monitor the temperature —most candy thermometers show 400°F. at the extreme upper end of their range. The mixture will liquefy at about 350°F.; but if it is poured at this temperature, air bubbles unable to rise to the surface will be trapped in the resin. If you allow the mixture to become too hot it will discolor to shades of amber and brown.

Pour the resin around the mold, letting it flow over the whole surface to a depth of about 3/16″. Be very careful with the hot resin. Dropping or splashing a 400° liquid could be disastrous.

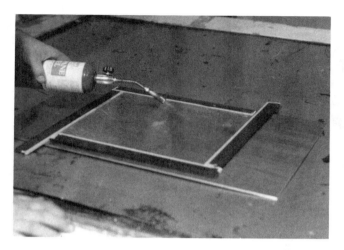

Use a propane torch or a heat gun to spot-heat sections where air bubbles have been caught in the resins. Use gentle heat and keep the torch moving so the resin does not burn. It is entertaining to watch these air bubbles disappear, and the face shine clear and bright, as you tease the surface with a propane torch.

Be patient. Allow the casting time to cool slowly. When the resin has cooled enough to become solid, move the pane from the prepared table and allow it an hour or so to come down to room temperature.

As soon as the pane is cool enough to touch comfortably, you can remove it from the mold. Gently wiggle the retainers away one at a time from the still-warm windowpane.

Lift the pane from the table and peel away the cellophane.

If at any point in this casting process the windowpane should break, all that has been wasted is time. The broken pieces can be re-heated and re-poured. Better luck next time!

Repeated heating of the broken pieces will gradually darken the resin, however. Crystal-clear, transparent windowpanes must be cast from a batch of resin that is primarily fresh stock. Discolored pieces can be used in casting breakaway bottles, as shown on the next few pages.

Breakaway Bottles

The resins used in making breakaway window glass and bottles are not new. Motion picture studios have been using these breakaway items for many years. The factor that has been greatly improved with time, and that has made these resins useful to the average prop shop, is the mold in which the resins are poured.

Previously, the best mold for casting breakaway resin was a mold made of stainless steel. Not every shop has the capability of making stainless steel molds. The introduction of silicone rubber as a molding medium has put the manufacture of breakaway bottles within reach of every prop shop.

Making a Silicone Rubber Mold

Begin by selecting a bottle to serve as the model for the copies you wish to make. We chose a half-pint gin bottle for this demonstration, but you might choose a bottle of an altogether different shape or size. Mix up two ounces of silicone rubber according to the manufacturer's directions and according to the instructions on silicone RTV rubber given earlier in this book (pages 55 to 60).

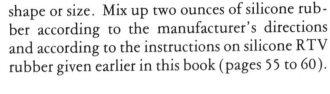

Paint the bottle with an impression coat of silicone rubber. Make this coating as thick as possible. Much of it will run down from the bottle and onto your working surface; scrape it up and put it back where it is needed. It will eventually begin to thicken and stay in place. Wait overnight for the silicone to cure.

Mix another batch of silicone rubber and give the bottle a second coat. Lay some stretch-weave fabric into the wet silicone. The silicone will soak into the loose weave and stay in place much more cooperatively than the first coating did.

Apply more liquid rubber, filling the fabric with as much as it will retain. Wait overnight for the silicone to cure.

Make a plaster mother mold to hold the silicone in its proper shape: Build a box a little larger than the bottle; grease it with petroleum jelly or liquid soap; pour it half full with plaster of Paris.

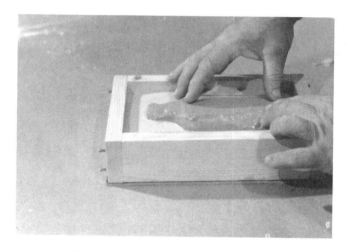

Lay the silicone-covered bottle in the wet plaster and press down till it is exactly half submerged. The bottle may tend to float. Hold it in place till the plaster firms up a little.

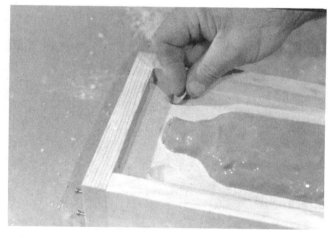

Use a coin or a large washer to gouge out a keying notch. Make one of these depressions in each corner of this first half of the mold.

Apply a release agent (petroleum jelly or liquid soap) to the exposed plaster, and pour the second half of the mother mold.

Shape and smooth the outside of the mold with a wide-blade putty knife. Let the entire mold cure overnight.

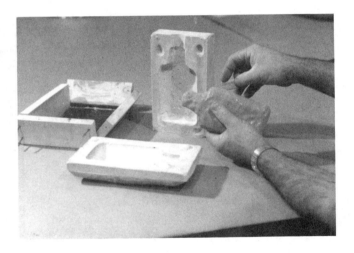

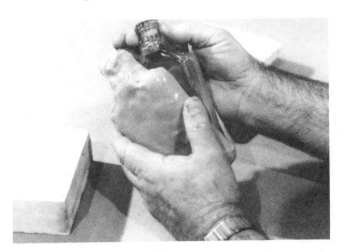

Remove the box, separate the plaster mother mold, and extract the rubber-covered bottle. Open the mouth of the bottle with a razor blade. Completely cut away from the mouth any rubber that might later obstruct resin being poured into the mold.

Slit the silicone mold down the edge with a sharp razor blade. This slit will create a faint seamline flaw in your castings, but it is necessary for removal of your pattern now and for the subsequent removal of your castings.

Remove the bottle gently, taking care not to tear the silicone mold.

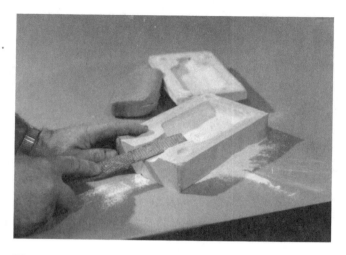

Use a coarse-toothed wood rasp to make an opening in the top of the mother mold. Make this opening widest at the outside of the mother mold, and it will act as a funnel.

Re-seat the silicone rubber mold in its plaster housing. Hold the mother mold together with a rubber restraint, and your mold is ready to use.

As you make a series of picco resin castings from the same mold, you may notice that after the first few pourings, the quality of the castings improves. A mold at room temperature is too cool for the best casting results, causing the castings to cool too quickly. You can remedy the problem somewhat by preheating the plaster mother mold. Heat the plaster mold to about 120°F. in a kiln or gas oven. Don't let the plaster get *too* hot—after all, you must handle this mold.

Making the Breakaway Casting

Mix a batch of picco resin as outlined in the foregoing section on breakaway window panes, using the same care to protect yourself from the danger of burns.

Fill the prepared mold with liquid resin. Pour the resin against one edge of the plaster "funnel" rather than straight down the middle of the mold. By flowing into the bottle this way, the resin churns up fewer air bubbles. It's analogous to pouring beer down the side of a glass to produce less head.

Wait five minutes or so for the resin lining the mold to cool slightly and form a thin shell. Then pour all the resin that is still liquid back into the heating pot.

The plaster mother mold is an insulator, holding in a great deal of heat. The resins clinging to the sides of the rubber mold are thickening but are still in a molten state; they will retain a tendency to sag and run for a little while. Stand the mold upright with its mouth down for the next half hour, allowing free drainage. If you rest the mold on its side during this cooling period, the "upper" side will become disfigured with sags and the "lower" side will become thick.

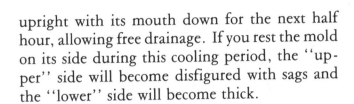

After the mold has been standing inverted for thirty to forty-five minutes, you can lay it down (gently) and remove the top half of the mother mold. Allowing the bottle to cool slowly minimizes the likelihood of cold shock and premature breakage.

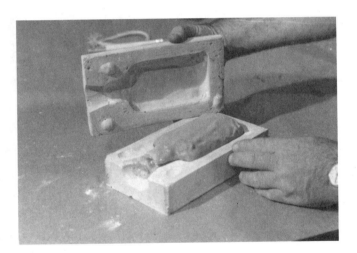

When the silicone rubber mold has cooled sufficiently to be comfortable to the touch, it can be opened. Lift the flaps of the rubber mold slowly and gently, releasing the casting from its confinement. When the casting is completely unencumbered, lift it out.

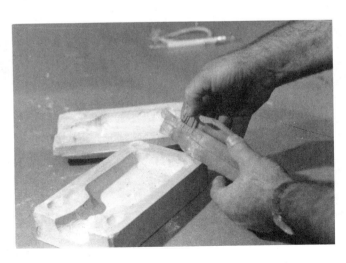

Here are the original gin bottle, the mold, and three castings.

THERMOSETS

A large group of plastics find a kinship in the fact that they solidify into a permanent shape when a catalyst is mixed with a primary liquid resin. The chemical activity triggered by the catalyst produces heat and cures the plastic; thus the generic name "thermoset." Thermosets differ from hot melts (thermoplastics) in that the thermosetting process is not reversible—that is to say, once the plastic has cured, it cannot be reheated and recycled.

The great variety of plastics belonging to this family makes it difficult to package and present them in a single orderly arrangement in this handbook; instead, they are scattered throughout the manual. Mold-making rubber (silicone RTV) and polyester resin (an essential ingredient in fiberglass) have already been introduced (silicone RTV on pages 55 to 60, fiberglass and polyester resin on pages 109 to 115). Another branch of the family tree will be examined in the upcoming section on Urethane Casting Materials (pages 147 to 160). Plastic body filler, a close relative of polyester resin, will be discussed in the section on Casting with Hardware Store Products (pages 165 to 168).

The most widely used thermoset—polyester resin—will be further dealt with here, as we make castings of chandelier pendants and of wood mouldings.

Safety Considerations

Most thermosets contain chemicals that are outright toxic. This statement is especially true when it comes to polyester resins and the catalyst used to trigger their cure. To put it plainly, do not allow these chemicals to come in contact with your skin, eyes, or lungs.

Four very important paragraphs on the safe use of polyester resin appear in this handbook in the discussion of fiberglass under Laminated Castings. The product used for making polyester castings, as outlined on the next few pages, is almost identical to the resin used for fiberglass laminations. Please refer to pages 109 and 110 for detailed safety precautions, all of which apply here. To repeat the summary:

SUMMARY: Do not breathe the fumes of uncured polyester resin. Work in a space that is supplied with forced ventilation, and wear a well-fitting and approved vapor respirator. Wear goggles when handling and mixing MEK peroxide; wear rubber gloves when working with the catalyst or liquid resin. Mix the catalyst according to the manufacturer's directions. Do not work in the presence of sparks or flames.

Polyester Resin

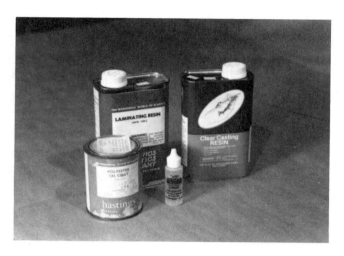

Three forms of polyester resin are readily available—laminating resin, gel coat, and casting resin. All three are chemically very similar, and each is activated by the same catalyst—MEK peroxide.

Casting resin contains as one of its ingredients a wax that rises to the surface during the curing process to provide a smooth tack-free finish to the casting. You might infer from that statement that *laminating* resin does not have wax in its recipe, and that the cured lamination has a sticky surface—and you would be right.

There are four distinct stages that polyester resins go through in their metamorphosis from liquid to solid. First, there is the gel stage, which occurs somewhere between ten minutes and sev-

eral hours after casting, depending on the product and the amount of catalyst used. At this point the liquid becomes gelatinous, no longer runny. Next comes the exothermic period. The gel becomes warm (or hot), and it gets firmer. This stage ends as the casting cools; in a few more hours the casting reaches maximum hardness. The final phase that nearly all resins go through is a period of shrinkage which takes place about a day later.

If you find that a casting is so firmly attached to a mold that it won't release without breakage, you might wait a couple of days to see if the eventual shrinkage of the casting makes the separation possible. (This suggestion applies only when you are casting in a negative mold. A casting laminated over a positive mold can only cling more tenaciously as it shrinks.)

Liquid casting resin has a slight violet tint, but it is for all practical purposes clear when cast in thin cross sections. Dyes are available, both opaque and transparent, which can be added to polyester resin. It is a common practice, however, to cast untinted resin and then to paint the casting after it has been filled and sanded.

Fillers can be added to polyester resin to thicken, texture, extend, and in some cases (as with glass fibers) strengthen it. Cab-O-Sil is a commercially produced thickening agent; silica, sand, gypsum, and sawdust have also been used to help control the viscosity of the thin syrupy resin and

to change its texture. Any additive put into polyester resin, whether colorant or filler, will have an effect on the setting time—usually retarding it. Water or moisture allowed in the resin will inhibit curing and can sometimes ruin the batch.

A mold for a set of crystal pendants can be made from the same silicone RTV rubber described earlier in this manual (pages 55 to 60). This time, however, the mold can be poured solid and still remain economical because of its low volume. The 1/4" walls are thick enough to be structurally sound, and no mother mold is needed.

The project illustrated here was for a chandelier

with seventy-five pendants. Making a mold that could accommodate five pendant castings at a time, we were able to produce the required number of pendants in fifteen pourings of the resin.

The original glass patterns were borrowed from an authentic chandelier. They were not harmed and were returned to the source, with no one the wiser.

Making the Mold

Make a little box to house the five original glass patterns. The box should be about ¼″ bigger in each direction than the glass pendant. Also allow ¼″ clearance between each pair of crystals.

Provide a rod across the top of the mold so the patterns can be freely suspended from their attachment wires. If necessary, bend the attachment wires so the pendants are aligned in a neat parallel row.

Pouring the Silicone

Mix the silicone as outlined in the section on "Silicone Molds." Pour enough liquid rubber to fill the box halfway, and then re-align the pendants to be certain they remain parallel. Pour in more silicone, this time filling the box to its brim. Allow the silicone to cure for about twelve hours.

Opening the Mold

Remove the box. Press on the sides of the mold with your fingers to locate the edges of the glass patterns. Use a razor blade to cut carefully through the rubber to the edge of each glass pattern. The slit will leave a faint seam line in your castings, but it will be almost invisible if you manage to keep your razor cut on the exact edge of each crystal.

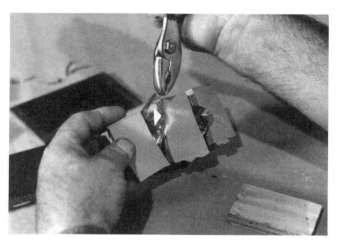

Pry the original patterns from the flexible rubber mold. The wires will be embedded in the silicone at the point of attachment to the rod. You will have to free the wires with the razor blade, but don't worry about chewing up the mold above the pendants. Any disfigurement there will be trimmed away when you cut pouring holes into the top of each pendant.

When all patterns have been removed, wrap several rubber bands around the mold to secure it.

Polyester casting resin is transparent when it cures. It produces a copy which has a smooth, tack-free surface; and though it is not as clear as glass, it is a reasonably good substitute.

This resin is formulated very much like the laminating resin demonstrated in the section on

Fiberglass (pages 109 to 115). It uses the same catalyst and mixes in almost the same ratio as the resin described there. Mix the casting resin with its catalyst according to the directions that come with the product you are using. The material we used for this project recommended seven drops of catalyst per ounce of resin when the mass of the casting is this small. Stir the mixture thoroughly.

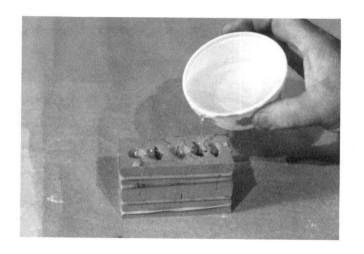

You can see the little funnels that were cut into the top of each cavity in the mold. This was done with a razor blade.

Pour the resin slowly, making a very small stream of fluid. If you attempt to pour too fast, air bubbles will impede the flow. Fill each chamber in turn, refilling if necessary when air escapes.

Let the castings cure undisturbed for four to five hours. It is unlikely that an appreciable amount of heat will be released by the curing of a casting this small.

When the casting has had time to cure it can be removed from the mold. The castings separate from the silicone mold even more easily than the original patterns did.

WATER-EXTENDABLE POLYESTER (WEP)

In a world where water contamination will ruin a batch of polyester, it is surprising that you can find a polyester resin that is designed to accept water into its chemistry. Water, stirred into the mixture by the user, extends the volume of this resin and actually improves its strength. The water does not immediately unite with the resin, but is dispersed throughout the liquid in the form of minute droplets. When the catalyst is added and the cure begins, the union is consummated as these tiniest of globules form the basis of crystals.

Making a WEP Casting

A WEP casting can be made from any of the molding materials covered in this manual, even plaster, providing the proper release agents are utilized. The project illustrated below and on the next page uses the alginate mold that we took from a bureau drawer decoration; that molding was demonstrated in the section on Moulage (pages 48 to 50).

No mold release is needed when you cast WEP in a moulage mold.

Mixing the WEP

Calculate how much casting material you will need. The casting illustrated here will take a very small amount of mixed resin — about 40 milliliters. We decided to mix resin and water in a 3:1 ratio (the manufacturer says the water content can be as high as 1:1).

We poured about 30 ml of the resin into a clean container, added five drops of MEK peroxide to the small batch, and then added 10 ml of tap water.

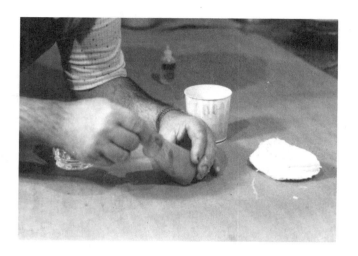

A thorough mixing of ingredients is always important, and it's especially important with WEP. Use a clean wooden stick (Popsicle stick or tongue depressor) to stir a small amount such as we have here. If you are mixing a batch with a larger volume, it might be helpful to use an electric mixer to ensure that the water is completely dispersed. As the mixture is stirred, the brown resin takes on a creamy consistency.

Pouring the Casting

Pour the catalyzed resin into the mold, completely filling it.

The casting should enter the gelatinous stage within ten minutes and be through the heat stage within a total of about twenty minutes. You can separate the casting from the mold and begin another pouring immediately. Even though an alginate mold has a short life, you should be able to cast ten or twelve copies before the mold deteriorates.

The casting can be glued to the drawer facings or drilled and put in place with small nails or screws.

If you should want stronger castings, chopped fiberglass strands could be added to the resin before the catalyst is added. This additive changes the viscosity of the resin; the mixture will likely have to be spooned into the mold and the mold jiggled to level out the casting.

URETHANE CASTING MATERIALS

Polyurethanes are packaged as casting materials in several different forms. Each formulation gives the plastic a unique set of physical characteristics. Urethane plastics can take the form of a light-weight foam, either flexible or rigid. You'll find flexible urethane foam in your bed mattress and in the cushions on your couch. The rigid foam is used as insulation inside the walls and door of your refrigerator; it also turns up every year at Christmastime, cut into those little spheres that are popular among those who like to make their own tree ornaments.

Polyurethane casting resin is chemically similar to urethane foam, but its recipe includes no foaming agent; when it is cast there is no increase in volume and the casting remains solid. Urethanes can also be compounded to produce a flexible RTV material closely resembling rubber. With all this versatility, there are bound to be many occasions when polyurethane is the ideal casting choice for the property builder.

Urethane foam has been in use in the theater for nearly forty years; it was first known as a casting material whose two parts were mixed together and poured into puddles which rose to become free-form "rocks." It was also poured into the cavities of scenic platforms to muffle the hollow rumble of footsteps on wood. The properties shops poured the foam into baking pans to make prop cupcakes, pastries, and "fresh-baked" bread. In those days we were so fascinated by the wondrous effects of the expanding gases that many of us tended to overlook the fact that the gases were noxious.

Safety Considerations

In the last twenty years much has been learned about the chemistry of polyurethanes; the most potentially harmful of the poisons — the carcinogens — have been designed out of the products. However, this does not mean that polyurethanes can be used without caution. The present formulation is still considered to be toxic and must be handled with care and with specific safeguards. Do not allow these products to come in contact with your body. Hands must be protected with a barrier cream or rubber gloves and should be given a thorough scrubbing after a job is completed. Polyurethanes must never be used in an enclosed space, but in an environment that is well ventilated. People with allergies or with a history of cardiac or respiratory difficulties should not be exposed even briefly to the chemicals used in polyurethane resins. Anyone is likely to develop an allergic sensitivity if exposed to direct contact with these chemicals.

SUMMARY: Do not breathe the fumes of polyurethane resins. Work in an air space supplied with forced ventilation, and wear a well-fitting and approved vapor respirator. Wear goggles to protect your eyes from splashed liquids. Wear latex gloves to protect yourself from skin contact with the resins. Do not work in the presence of sparks or flame.

These hazard precautions read a lot like those of polyester resins. The dangers are similar, even though the chemistry of the materials is very different.

Polyurethane and the Special Need for Mold Release

Polyurethane in all its forms has a tragic character flaw: it is so tenacious that it just *will not* separate from a plaster mold. Yet there are those who say that plaster molds *can* be used when they are properly prepared. Let me share the wisdom of these "others."

It has been explained to me that the secret is in the preparation of the plaster mold. Those who have had success agree that these are the requirements:

1. The plaster mold must be newly cast. It must be fresh, dry, and unused, with a smooth surface.

2. The mold should be sealed. The consensus of these mold makers is that two light coats of lacquer (with drying time after each coat) will do the job.

3. The sealed mold must be coated with repeated applications of PVA (with drying time after each application).

4. When the PVA has set up and dried well, it should be coated with paste wax. The wax should be buffed.

Two-Part Urethane Foam

There is a system used by some shops of casting urethane foam in small-necked two-part plaster molds. When the foam is thus cast, there is a point at which the foam begins to issue from the mouth of the mold. The mold is then capped tightly, and pressure builds up inside the mold. This pressure makes the cells of the foam dense and smooth against the walls of the plaster mold. When the casting is removed from the mold, it is in the form of an extremely lightweight object with a smooth surface. I can testify to having seen such castings, to having spoken with those who made them, and to having destroyed several well-made plaster molds in attempts to reproduce the results in our shop. Unfortunately, I am unable to illustrate the process here, as I have never been successful with it.

When we cast polyurethane in our shop, we use silicone molds. Urethane foam adheres to everything; silicone RTV rubber releases cleanly from everything. In a tug-of-war between the two materials, silicone rubber's repellent quality wins over polyurethane's grasp.

I have found rigid two-part polyurethane foam to be of great value in making vacuum-form patterns. When a vacuum-formed styrene casting is filled with this rigid foam, the foam provides strength against collapse, and the filled shell can then be used as a pattern to make additional vacuum-formed copies. This process will be explored in the chapter on Vacuum-Forming with Thermoplastics (pages 172 to 209).

Flexible Urethane Foam Castings

I would be forced to write another paragraph like the earlier one on rigid urethane foam in a plaster mold, this time describing my failures with *flexible* urethane foam, if I had not been introduced to a beautifully simple little procedure. This technique overcomes all of my objections about urethane foam clinging to everything.

Before you pour the two-part foam, lay a skin of latex rubber in your mold. The urethane will stick with its reliable fervor to the latex skin . . .

but the latex will separate easily from the plaster mold. (I have recently discovered that the same technique is applicable to rigid urethane foam. However, the seal between the latex skin and the plaster mold must be broken and the skin replaced before the foam is poured.)

We will demonstrate the process by making a flexible wine bottle (for an altercation in *La Quinta de Pancho Diablo*) and a realistic replica of a fish (for a production of *The Tender Trap*).

Pouring the Latex Skin

Use a freshly poured plaster mold—one that is dry, has not been sealed, and is not contaminated. A mold release is not absolutely necessary, but a light dusting of talcum powder will be helpful in facilitating a separation.

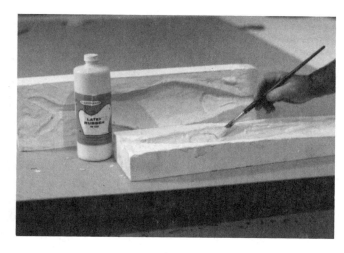

Coat the interior of the mold with latex. This can be accomplished by pouring in enough latex to fill the mold halfway and manipulating the mold in your hands, allowing the liquid to flow over all parts of the mold surface; then pouring the surplus latex back into its container...

...or you can simply use a brush to dab a heavy coating of latex over the inner surfaces of the mold halves. In either case, allow an eight-hour period for the latex to dry.

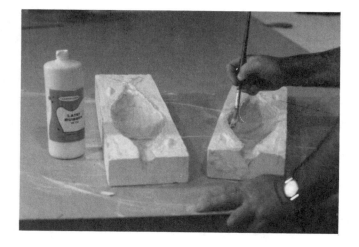

Liberally coat the seamline with a fresh application of latex.

Clamp the mold halves together while the latex on the seamline is still liquid. When the mouth of a mold is as small as those of the molds we are using here, there is so little room for air to circulate into and out of the mold that the latex may take an inconveniently long time to dry. This drying time can be shortened by forcing air circulation. Our method was to connect a hairdryer to a small-diameter rubber hose and to use this assemblage to blow cool air into the mold. The hose should be large enough to permit free flow of air but small enough so that it does not seal the mouth of the mold—the air must be allowed an escape route. With the hose pushed deep into the mold, the forced-air circulation will dry the latex.

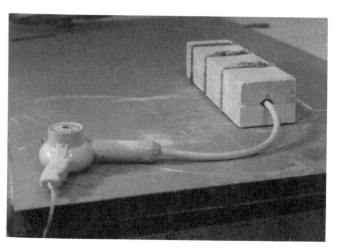

Most manufacturers provide a choice of urethane foam products; these are available in both rigid and flexible forms, and both forms can be obtained in at least two foam densities—usually four and eight pounds per cubic foot. The four-pound urethane foam expands to a greater volume and is therefore lighter. The cells formed in the eight-pound foam are smaller and packed more tightly together; this makes the eight-pound foam denser, heavier, and stronger. We used the four-pound foam in the projects illustrated on the following pages.

Mixing the Foam Ingredients

Mix the two parts of the urethane foam kit according to the mixing directions that come with it. You may be instructed to mix proportions by either weight or volume; whatever the instructions direct you to do, *be exacting*. This is not a plastic in which a catalyst simply triggers a reaction; these ingredients, in specific proportions, interact chemically to make a new compound. Inaccurately measured ingredients will leave uncombined chemicals in the foam and will weaken the final product.

The product we used in this demonstration is to be mixed in a ratio of 38:100 by weight. The first step is usually to weigh the empty container and take this weight into account in calculating the mixture proportions.

Our scale can be "zeroed"—it can be made to adjust automatically for the weight of the empty cup. If your scale does not have this feature, you will have to subtract the weight of your container from each reading you take. In other words, if your cup weighs 15 g and you want to weigh out 100 g of the first chemical, the scale must read 115 g on this first weighing.

Pour the desired quantity of the chemical designated part "A." We chose to use 100 g of the first part—not only because this figure makes it easy to calculate proportions, but because experience has shown us that this quantity will expand to almost a quart, the approximate amount needed for this project.

Next add the correct amount of the chemical designated part "B." In the photo we have poured part "B" into the cup till the scale indicated 138 g.

Stirring and Pouring the Urethane

Stir the two parts together immediately and rapidly. As soon as the mixture begins to froth — this will happen within fifteen to twenty seconds — pour it into the latex-lined mold.

As you watch, the foam will rise and grow warm.

The next step in the operation may be the most difficult for you (it is for many people). *You must leave the mold absolutely undisturbed for at least half an hour.* Don't touch it. Don't move it. Don't bump the table. Don't slam the door. The situation is analogous to one you may recall, when your mother or grandmother would bake a cake; any jarring of the mold will cause the casting to "fall," until the fragile cells containing the expanded gases have cured and become firm.

Opening the Mold

When the polyurethane has cured, open the mold. Use a knife blade to pry the halves apart. You may have to turn the mold over and pry from the other side, and then return to the first side; if you exercise persistence, the plaster halves will separate. Then there is no trick to peeling the flexible casting from the mold.

Treating the Seam

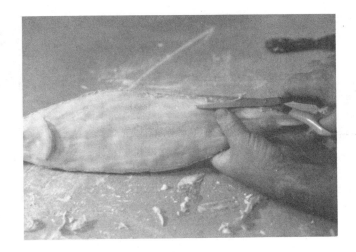

The seam of the casting can be cleaned up with a pair of scissors.

Brush a little liquid latex onto the seam and blend it into the surrounding rubber. There is a very thin liquid latex rubber available from R&D Latex (the product is called R&D 625) which is of balloon quality. Repeated applications of this latex will help to blend out the seam lines.

Supplemental Techniques Useful When Working with Latex and Urethane

Putting Fins on the Fish

The casting of the fish will look a lot more convincing if it is "dressed up" with fins, gills, and

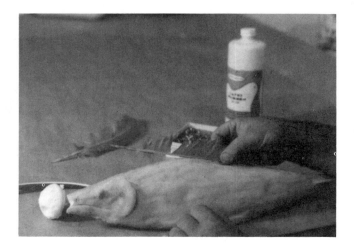

a paint job that accentuates the scales. Fins can be simulated with a chicken or turkey feather.

Split the feather down the middle of its shaft with a utility knife. Hold half of the split feather against the "spine" of the fish to determine an appropriate length for the dorsal fin. Cut the feather to size.

Dip the cut feather in liquid latex. Then, using the latex as an adhesive, attach the feather where it is needed. Keep the latex-coated feather in

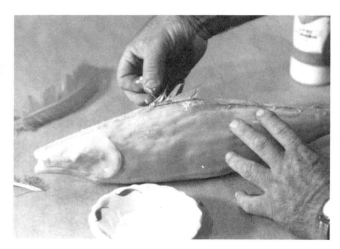

place till the latex dries by pushing pins through it and into the urethane foam body of the fish.

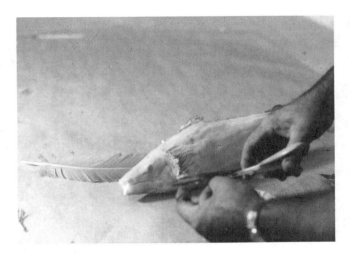

Attach a feathery appendage to the rear edge of the gills.

Secure a latex-coated feather to the trailing edge of the tail also.

Painting a Latex Casting

The flexing and stretching qualities of latex rubber make it especially difficult to color. Most paints sold commercially cannot expand and contract with the latex skin. They tend to form flakes and fall off. You can make a rubber-based paint yourself, however, that is very successful on latex.

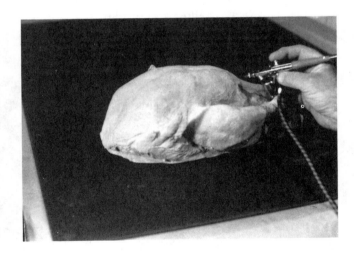

Here are the components of the flexible paint:

1. Rubber cement—the kind used for cementing paper. This is the paint's flexible binder.

2. Universal tinting colors—available in tubes from artists' suppliers. These can be mixed to provide a wide range of colors.

3. Naphtha—the solvent, used for thinning the paint to a useful consistency and for cleanup.

When the paint has been prepared, it can be sprayed on with an airbrush or applied with a paintbrush.

Hair Implanting

Another technique that is neither molding nor casting, but directly related to them, is the implanting of hair in a latex skin.

The puppet head shown below was reproduced using the technique described a few pages

earlier, of casting flexible polyurethane in a latex skin (pages 149 to 153). (The construction of the mold was shown on pages 40 to 42 under Two-Part Mold — Shim Method.)

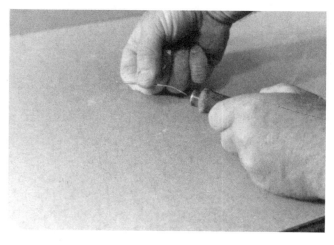

Make a hair-implanting tool by forcing a large upholstery or tent-maker's needle into a wooden handle. Push the point of the needle deep into the wood.

Use a pair of diagonal pliers to cut off the tip of the needle's eye. This will leave a sharp two-pointed fork on the exposed end of the needle.

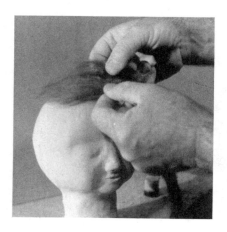

Spread open a section of crepe hair. Lay a fine mat of this hair on the doll's head. Make yourself oblivious to the gruesome aspect of the activity, and repeatedly jab your forked tool through the mat of crepe hair and into the doll's head. Each jab will take a few strands of hair with it and

firmly root them in the doll's scalp.

By using care and patience (sometimes working one hair at a time), it is possible to achieve very delicate and lifelike effects which bear up very well under close scrutiny — even by a close-up lens.

Urethane RTV Casting Rubber

Another in the family of urethane casting materials is urethane RTV casting rubber. It forms a flexible solid (not a foam) and can be purchased under a number of commercial names including "Ad-rub" and "Devcon." This plastic is ideal for casting low-relief decorations, headdress ornamentations, knobs, baubles, bangles ...yes, even beads, if they don't have to be bright and shiny. Most manufacturers of urethane RTV rubber make the product available in several degrees of resilience, from soft to firm. In the project that follows we have illustrated the production of a knife handle using one of the firmer formulations.

Selecting the Model

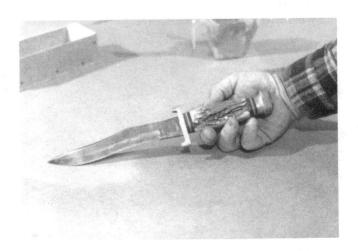

This knife has an interesting bone handle that spans hundreds of years. It would look equally suitable in the hands of Coriolanus and Daniel Boone.

Making the Mold

Mix a batch of silicone rubber to make a mold from the original knife handle. Mix the silicone rubber according to the manufacturer's specifications; refer to the detailed instructions given in the section of this book that deals with Silicone RTV Rubber Molds (pages 55 to 60).

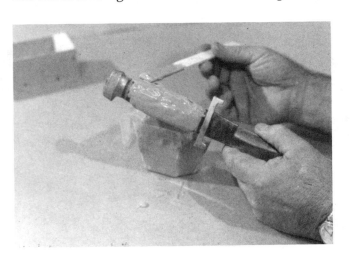

Use an expendable paint brush or a wooden spatula to apply a thin impression coating of silicone rubber over the whole knife handle. Carefully cover all parts of the handle, allowing no air pockets to remain. Set the knife aside to cure for twelve hours.

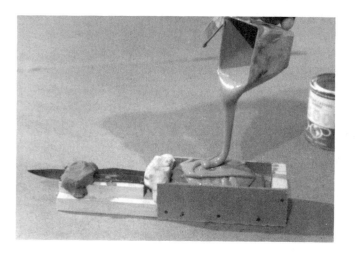

A small box of pine and Masonite will control the silicone rubber as it is being poured. The box should be larger than the pattern by about ¼″ in every direction.

Support the weight of the knife by holding the blade in place so that the handle is suspended ¼″ above the floor of the box. Seal the opening where the knife enters the box with wax-based modeling clay.

Pour the silicone till the form is filled to the brim, and set the assemblage aside for another twelve hours.

When the rubber has cured, slit the mold to allow the pattern to be removed easily. The incision in the mold will inevitably leave a seam line in the reproduction. Be careful to make this cut only as extensive as is necessary to allow the pattern's release.

Making a Blade

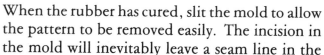

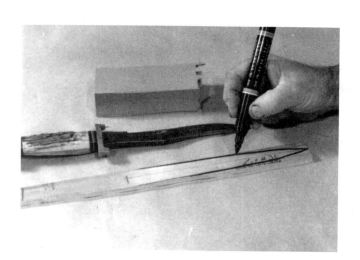

Make a knife blade from a piece of ³⁄₁₆″ flat sill iron or aluminum stock. Allow extra length in order for the blade to extend the full length of the hilt.

Mixing the Urethane RTV Casting Rubber

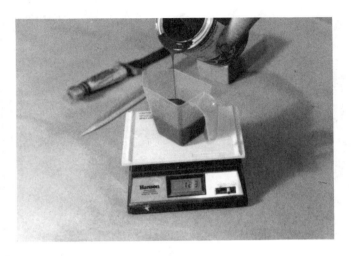

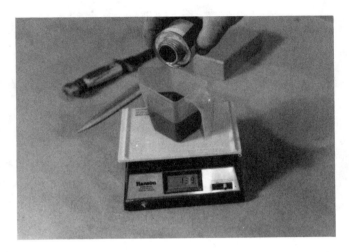

Urethane RTV casting rubber must be mixed in precise proportions; each of the chemicals is integral to the final compound. Part "B" is not merely a catalyst; and unlike certain polyester resins, using a greater concentration of part "B" in the mix will not cause the plastic to set faster. An excess of either chemical will be unable to enter into the desired chemical reaction and ultimately will act as a contaminant, resulting in an inferior batch. Mix the parts as you are instructed by the manufacturer. The ratio of the two parts is usually computed by weight, although some manufacturers specify proportions by volume. In either case, measure carefully; if you use a scale, don't forget to allow for the weight of the measuring cup.

Preparing the Mold and Pouring the Resin

You can keep a mold of this size closed tightly by wrapping it with rubber bands. The pressure supplied by this restraint is sufficient to prevent leakage at the seam. Pour the prepared urethane RTV rubber compound into your mold.

The natural tendency of urethane RTV is to hold fast to any surface it has contact with before it cures; silicone rubber, however, has no affinity for such an embrace. In this chemical battle of wills, silicone's repellency wins—therefore no mold release is necessary.

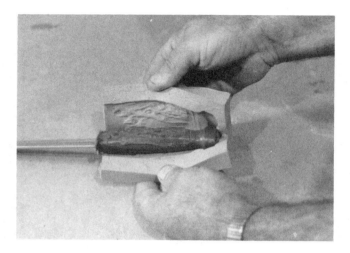

Insert your prepared knife blade into the exact center of the liquid urethane mixture. The urethane, as one would expect, will cling tenaciously to the knife blade.

Provide a support to retain this absolute uprightness while the urethane rubber cures. We held our blade vertical by adhering it to the side wall of a cabinet with a wad of Plasticine clay.

Allow the urethane rubber to set up overnight. When the casting has cured, remove the rubber-band restraints and peel the mold open to remove your reproduction.

CASTING WITH HARDWARE STORE PRODUCTS

The preceding chapters outline techniques for using materials specially designed for particular molding or casting needs. Many of these quality products are not readily available and must be ordered from the manufacturer or jobber—not necessarily a retailer. Unfortunately, sometimes these sources will be located in a city miles from your workplace.

It can therefore be handy to know about some molding and casting materials that are found

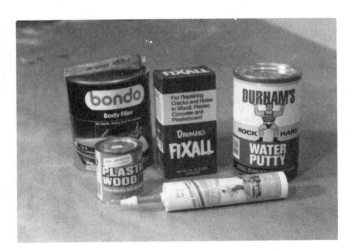

right on the shelves of your local hardware store. These products can be purchased at a moment's notice and may serve your needs without the inconvenient delay of a special order. Fortunately, casting plaster can usually be obtained locally in a lumberyard or in a paint or hardware store. The following pages will introduce some plastic products that are marketed for use as caulking, putty, and fillers, but can be useful in making molds and producing castings.

You could use an automobile repair plastic filler (Bondo) or your choice of three different spackling and putty products (Plastic Wood, Dowman's Fixall, and Durham's Rock Hard Water Putty) for making castings.

Silicone caulking can be used to make flexible molds.

And, of course, petroleum jelly and liquid soap have already been introduced as time-honored release agents, both readily available.

Silicone Caulking as a Mold-Making Material

Silicone caulking is a product that you can buy from almost any hardware store. It is a clear, flexible caulking sealer manufactured for use in filling cracks around windows and doors to make them airtight. This same product can also be used to make flexible molds. *Do not use white bathtub caulk.* It is not the same material.

Don't confuse this caulking material with silicone RTV rubber, which was explained earlier in this book. Silicone RTV rubber is a two-part mix (rubber and catalyst) which vulcanizes at room temperature, is rather expensive, and probably has the best reproductive characteristics of

any casting material. Clear silicone caulking is air drying and inexpensive and, even though it can be effective, it is a marginal entry on the list of mold-making materials.

Silicone caulking cures in the open air to produce a fairly tough, flexible skin. Curing takes place as the solvent, acetic acid, is removed from the compound. It is a curious chemical fact that the drying must take place in a slightly humid atmosphere. The acetic acid interacts with the moisture in the air. (This is of special concern to those living in the desert.)

Safety Considerations

Silicone caulking should be used in a ventilated space. The fumes of the solvent can be irritating to the membranes in your nose and lungs. Skin contact with acetic acid can also be irritating. Read and observe all warnings printed on the tube of caulking.

A Man for All Seasons has the historical figure Sir Thomas More in the title role. The chain of office worn by More is familiar to us because it is depicted in Hans Holbein's well-known portrait of the statesman; you may wish to reproduce this detail to augment and authenticate the character's costume.

Preparing the Pattern

Making the Mold

Select a product for mold-making which is clearly marked as being 100% silicone rubber. Some caulking compounds contain additives intended

SUMMARY: Use silicone caulk in a space that has good comfortable air movement. Before handling this material, apply a barrier cream to your hands. When your job is finished, wash your hands.

The construction of the necklace as demonstrated on the following pages utilizes nothing more exotic than hardware store products. The mold for the segments will be made of silicone caulking, and the individual links will be cast with plastic body filler.

Carefully sculpt one of the *S*-shaped links from Plasticine. Coat it with a thin application of petroleum jelly. Silicone caulking adheres to almost all surfaces, even glass; so a little petroleum jelly is helpful here. Spread on a very light coat that completely covers the pattern.

to retard the curing process and keep the sealant in a liquid state under the surface skin for a long time; these do not make good molds.

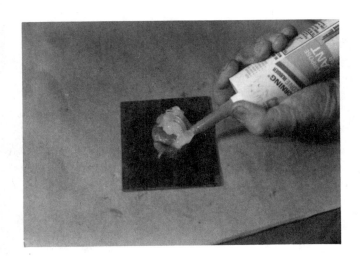

Cover the pattern with a liberal coat of silicone caulking. Apply the compound in a thick, even coating, and try to make the application as smooth as you can. Silicone caulking is translucent, so thin spots will show up as clear areas. Add more caulking to these spots till you have the pattern covered uniformly.

As soon as the caulking is exposed to the air it will begin to cure.

In an hour or so a skin will form over the surface, allowing you to pat the surface gently with your finger. This greatly improves the surface smoothness of the mold.

Completion of this decorative chain—casting of the links and their final assembly—will be discussed below under the heading ''Casting with Plastic Body Filler.'' Before we continue with this project, however, let's examine a few considerations peculiar to silicone caulking.

It may take as long as two or three days for a thick application of this caulking compound to fully air cure. A three-day wait is not time effi-cient—you might as well have phoned in an or-der and had the superior product, silicone RTV rubber, shipped to you. There is a way, however, to rush the cure time of silicone caulking: ex-posing it alternately to water and hot air. Spray the silicone-covered pattern with water; then work over the surface with a hair dryer. If this process is repeated several times in a twelve-hour period, the curing time can be cut to one day.

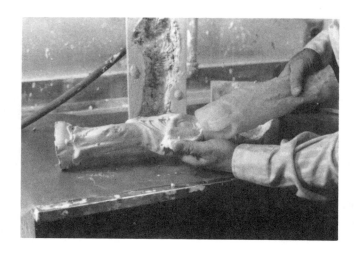

When silicone caulking is applied in a thin coating, a mold is produced which can peel back in the same manner as a latex rubber mold. Refer to the section in which latex rubber molds were demonstrated (pages 51 to 54) to see that material removed ''like a glove.''

Also like latex, thin-walled molds of flexible silicone caulking usually need a plaster mother mold to ensure that the correct shape is held.

Thin-walled molds of silicone caulking are only good for a few castings (eight to twelve) before they begin to tear. Molds with thicker walls (½") probably would not need a mother mold, and would still be flexible enough to separate easily from minor undercuts; but it takes much longer (up to a week) for these to cure. Here again, the time involved negates the efficiency of this molding material. The only real advantage of a silicone caulking mold, after all, is that the material is readily available on short notice. If you need only a few copies from a small original, you can produce them successfully from a mold of this material.

Casting with Plastic Body Filler

Plastic body filler is manufactured for use as a putty for making cosmetic repairs on the fenders and bodies of automobiles. The prop builder uses body putty in a similar way, making the surfaces of fiberglass castings smooth and free of flaws. This product has been recommended earlier in this book for use as a filler (as it was intended) in the section on casting with fiberglass. It adheres to almost everything, including metal, so it is a good medium for filling scars and imperfections on any object made of metal, wood, or fiberglass.

The manufacturers do not advertise this product as a casting material; but since its formulation has a base of polyester resin, it can be used to make durable castings of small objects. Mixed with a small amount of hardening agent, the putty becomes solid in a very short time.

Fillers are added by the manufacturer to the resin base to make it thick and workable. These fillers make the putty more viscous and keep it from running after it has been applied; they also help to make the plastic sandable. This is important to auto body men who use it, and you will find it important to you as you begin to do your sanding.

Safety Considerations

Plastic body filler is a form of polyester resin. You must observe all of the safeguards detailed earlier for use with polyester resin (see page 141).

Do not breathe the fumes released by the uncured putty. Uncured polyester resin is harmful when ingested, so take care not to get it in your mouth. The active ingredient in the cream hardener (the catalyst) is benzoyl peroxide. This catalyst is not nearly as corrosive as MEK peroxide, *but caution in using it is still appropriate. Do not smoke while using this product, and wash your hands when you have finished mixing and applying it.*

SUMMARY: Do not breathe the fumes of uncured polyester resin. Work in a space that is supplied with forced ventilation. Use barrier cream on your hands, and wash your hands when the job is done.

Mixing the Plastic Body Filler

Mix the putty according to the directions on the can. These instructions have become more or less standardized among the various manufacturers, so the auto-body men don't have to keep referring to the directions every time they open a can of the product with a different trade name. The standard instructions run something like this: "Add a one-inch ribbon of cream hardener to each fluid ounce of plastic. Mix till the coloring in the hardener is uniformly blended into the gray filler. Apply."

Some of these cream hardeners are colored burnt sienna (others are blue), and when the hardener is mixed with the plastic filler the mixture is a shade of pink (or blue). A pale pastel shade of the mixture sets up very slowly—it might take four hours or even a day for the putty to harden. A darker shade of putty will set up in ten or fifteen minutes and might become very hot in the process. With just a little practice you will learn to recognize the characteristics of a batch of putty just by assessing its coloring.

As promised, we are continuing with the chain necklace project begun a few pages ago.

Making the Casting

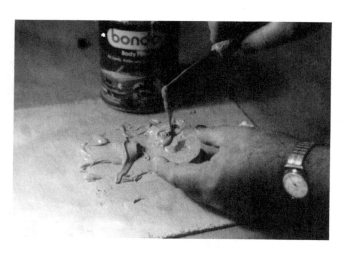

Fill the mold with putty. The putty is thick, but it should be liquid enough to flow into the contours of the mold. Tap the mold on the table top to shake the filler into all the crevices. Set the casting aside till it starts to become warm. This should be within fifteen minutes if the mixture was made with the right proportions.

Plastic body filler is designed for rapid production work in an auto body shop. If the catalyzed putty is properly mixed, you won't have a great deal of time to fuss with it. The plastic sets up in eight to ten minutes, so it is important that you mix only what you can use in this time span.

The mold can be flexed and the casting removed as soon as the plastic filler has reached its maximum heat.

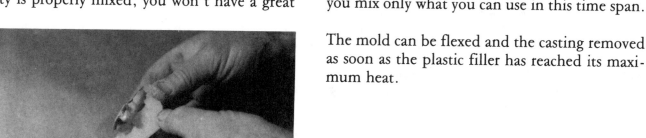

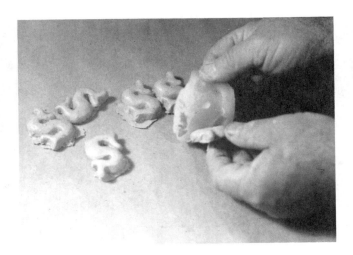

If you work with reasonable efficiency you should be able to turn out the castings at the rate of one every twenty minutes.

During the first stage of its cure the plastic will be firm but workable and can easily be carved with a knife. Later (in about an hour) it will have hardened to the consistency of a soft wood such as pine or fir, and although it can still be worked with a knife, this will have become more difficult, and it is best to shape the casting with sandpaper. When it is fully cured, the putty becomes even harder, like walnut or fruit wood.

It seems reasonable to digress briefly from the subject of casting to explain how to complete this impressive piece of jewelry.

The chain requires twenty-five of these *S*-shaped castings; so twenty-five wire frames are needed to link the castings together.

A bending jig for twisting the wire links will give assurance that all will be precisely alike. To make the jig, first draw a pattern on a piece of 2 × 4 fir. The dimensions of this pattern will be dictated by the size of your castings. We drew a square measuring 1¾" on each side. This allowed most of the wire to be hidden behind the casting, leaving exposed only the small circles of wire to be used for linking.

Drill a ¼" hole directly into the corner of the square, and drive a ¼" rod into each hole. Using soft iron or copper wire, wrap the posts to form a zig-zag *Z* shape as shown in the illustration. Make sure there is a complete circle at each corner of the *Z*. Clip the ends of the wires short and close the perfect circles with a pair of pliers if necessary.

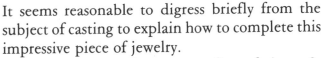

Hot-glue the wire frames to the *S*-shaped castings in such a way that the main wire shape is hidden from view. Only the ¼ʺ circles that allow linking should remain exposed. Join the individual links with an additional ¼ʺ ring of wire.

Here is the completed piece. The bottom link of the chain (the "three-legged" *S*) was cast separately; the pendant is a bauble that came from our junk jewelry drawer.

Castings made with Bondo have a natural coloring of pale burnt sienna. We sprayed our necklace so it would appear bronze with gold highlights.

Plastic Wood

Plastic Wood is a trade name for a cellulose fiber putty. There are other wood-dough products on the market that are similar, but Plastic Wood in particular has become the standard with puppeteers who use it as a casting material. It is designed to be used to fill rough spots and holes in wood. When Plastic Wood cures it assumes many qualities of soft wood: it can be glued, sawed, drilled, sanded, and tooled very much like a soft wood such as pine or fir. Plastic Wood cures as the solvent dries out of the putty.

Puppeteers have used Plastic Wood for casting puppet heads and bodies for at least thirty years. The techniques shown here are generally the same as those widely used by the puppeteers; but as there is sometimes disagreement on a technique that has evolved from tradition, the details that follow may draw criticism from those whose techniques vary slightly.

Safety Considerations

The solvent with which Plastic Wood is formulated—acetone or something very similar—is both volatile and highly flammable. Prolonged exposure to its fumes can cause dizziness and headache.

SUMMARY: Do not use near sparks or open flame. Work outdoors or in a space that is supplied with forced ventilation.

One of Plastic Wood's strong selling points as a wood putty is its ability to stick to a variety of different surfaces. Unfortunately, this includes your fingers and any protective gloves you might wear. A light coating of petroleum jelly rubbed onto your hands before you begin work will minimize (but not eliminate) this difficulty.

Mold Release

The first step in making a Plastic Wood casting is to dunk the mold in water. Surprised? The water will serve as a mold release. Keep the mold immersed for a four- to five-minute soaking.

It's O.K. to cast with a freshly-made plaster mold; the water trapped in fresh plaster can only be helpful. The mold in the illustration (from which we will cast an antique lock) was made the day before this photo was taken.

Taking the Casting

Make a silver dollar-sized pancake of the wood putty and press it into the plaster mold. Make another small pancake and overlap the edge of the preceding patch with it; press and smooth them till they blend together. Repeat this process till the entire interior surface of the mold is completely covered.

Press and blend the Plastic Wood in the mold till the walls of the casting are covered to a uniform thickness of about 3/16". Fragile areas such as the shackle of this lock should be filled almost solid, to add to the casting's strength.

Curing the Casting

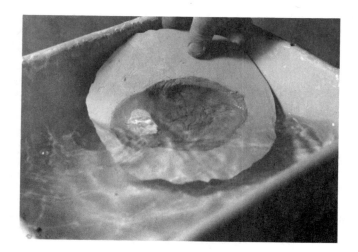

Submerge the plaster mold containing the Plastic Wood casting in a tub of water. If you've never worked with Plastic Wood before, this step will seem strange; but any puppet-maker will agree that it must be done. The point on which the puppeteers disagree is the length of time the mold should remain submerged—opinions run the gamut from ten minutes to two days. When you submerge the casting, air bubbles will begin to form as water replaces the air around the plaster crystals.

It is possible for the air bubbles to separate the casting from the mold, so keep an eye on the casting, and gently press the soft putty back in place if it comes loose.

This immersion serves two purposes. First, it saturates the plaster and ensures an easy separation when the casting has cured. Second, it slows the curing of the Plastic Wood. Plastic Wood shrinks as it cures, and the water bath reduces the amount of shrinkage. The advocates of the two-day dunking want the curing of the Plastic Wood to take place almost entirely under water.

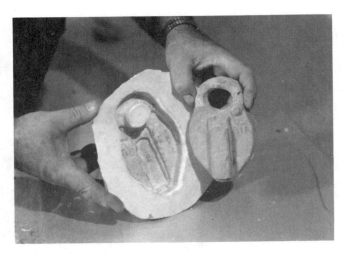

The Plastic Wood casting shown here was left under water for one hour and then was allowed to air dry for two days.

When Plastic Wood has cured its finish is not extremely rough, but it is not as smooth as some other casting materials. This lock, built to be attached to an "ancient" strongbox, was enhanced by the rough finish — it was intended to appear rusted and corroded. The shackle of this lock cannot be opened, of course; the staple on the strongbox was pried open to accept the lock.

Plastic Wood's similarity to wood does not end with its appearance. If a smooth finish is desired, it can be attained without too much attention. Just spackle and sand the surface.

Durham's Rock Hard Water Putty

Durham's Rock Hard Water Putty is very useful for filling large blemishes in wood. This is one putty that does not shrink as it hardens. It is sold as a powder, mixes with water, and works a lot like plaster. When it has cured, however, it has many of the characteristics of soft wood.

On this page we will demonstrate casting this material in a silicone rubber mold. The pattern for this casting was a wooden rosette, a typical Victorian decoration.

Mix the putty according to the instructions on the package. Add the powder to the appropriate volume of water—for this casting we used one cup of water. Keep adding powder and mixing till the mixture is barely pourable. (An overly thin mix of this putty has no strength.)

In almost every respect the prepared putty can be treated as if it were plaster. Pour the mold full . . .

. . . then joggle the mold to release any air bubbles that may be clinging to the inner surface of the mold, and set it aside to cure. As with plaster, a casting made of Durham's Rock Hard Putty will become firm in as little time as half an hour.

The finished casting is not as brittle as one cast from plaster would have been; it can be treated much as if it were made of wood.

Dowman's Fixall

Fixall is a very hard-setting putty, with some of the qualities of cement or mortar.

To use this product (as we have on this page),

follow the instructions on page 172 for Durham's Putty. The two products' characteristics differ, but the working procedures are almost identical.

The mold for this door knocker (or fountain ornament) was made of silicone rubber; a description of the mold-making process will be found in the section of this book that deals with Extending Silicone with Fillers (pages 70 to 73).

We have estimated that this casting will require about half a gallon of water. Keep adding powder to the water and stirring till a thick, pourable mixture is produced.

Pour the mixture into the mold.

For an object this size there is no reason that the casting must remain solid. Scooping a hol-

lowed depression in the side that will remain unseen will make the casting considerably lighter without sacrificing strength.

Opening the Mold

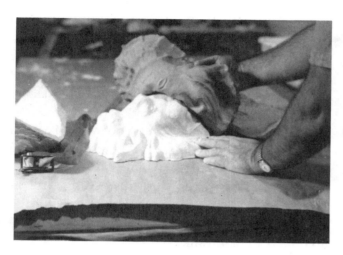

The casting should be firm in about half an hour, and after setting overnight the mold can be peeled away.

The metalwork for this door knocker was bent from a length of ½″ rod. Two large washers were welded in place to provide a grip and a rapping surface.

VACUUM FORMING WITH THERMOPLASTICS

Vacuum Forming Machines

Vacuum forming machines produce thin, light-weight, shell-like plastic castings. The machine has two basic parts—the oven and the forming platform. The oven portion of the machine heats a sheet of thermoplastic till it softens. Then atmospheric pressure forces the softened sheet snugly around a pattern on the forming table. When cooled to room temperature, the plastic holds its new shape, forming a strong, inexpensive, lightweight casting. If you design three-dimensional details into the surface of the pattern, this thin shell can be surprisingly strong.

Following the directions offered in Nick Bryson's *Thermoplastic Scenery for the Theater,* our shop crew built two vacuum forming machines, one with a 4′ × 4′ table and a smaller portable unit with a 2′ × 2′ table. On the following pages you will find a complete explanation of how to build the smaller unit. (The procedure is adaptable if you wish to construct a larger machine.) Then we demonstrate ways in which we have used both units. It is our hope that you will see additional possibilities for using a vacuum forming

machine already in your possession, and if you do not own one, that you may become inspired to build a machine of your own.

The vacuum forming machine must be used with imagination if you wish to attain its highest potential and make this tool cost-effective. A machine not used to its fullest can become a large, costly white elephant. When we built our vacuum forming machine in 1978, we were fortunate in having a group of MFA student designers eager to explore the new machine's possibilities.

We built our larger vacuum form first, assembling it in the UCLA properties shop. The overall dimensions of the table are such that we cannot remove it from that room without dismantling it. The properties shop, therefore, produces all the vacuum formed items used by our theater department. In the discussion of vacuum forming methods that follows, many references are made to the construction of large scenic items. The techniques of vacuum forming plastic, however, are exactly the same when you are producing smaller vacuum formed properties.

Vacuum Formable Plastics

There are several plastics available in sheet form that work well in the vacuum forming process. These include polyethylene, acrylic, styrene, cellulose acetate, and vinyl, among others. This allows you to choose from a wide variety of thicknesses, colors, and degrees of transparency.

In the UCLA shop we work almost exclusively with white high-impact polystyrene in one thickness—30 mil. Economy and a lack of storage prompted us to stick to one medium; it seems to

work for us. We get a pretty good price break when we buy in thousand-pound lots (about 350 4′ × 4′ sheets), and we don't have storage space to accommodate more than one size. When we must vacuum form an object in some other plastic or in thicknesses of polystyrene other than 30 mil, we special-order just enough to do the job. Because most of our experience has been so confined to 30 mil polystyrene, the illustrations and explanations that follow are based on that product.

The Vacuum Forming Process

A vacuum forming machine consists of two basic parts: an oven and a platen or forming table. The unit shown here has a "flip-flop" frame, one hinged to the main body of the machine. The frame quickly and accurately transfers the heated plastic from the oven to the forming table.

When you turn the machine on, two things happen. The oven begins to preheat, and a vacuum pump draws the air from a vacuum holding tank. When the vacuum in the tank reaches a predetermined level, a vacuum switch turns the pump off. Before forming the first sheet of plastic, let the oven preheat, with a lid in place, for about fifteen minutes. Preheating causes the entire oven bed to act as a radiator and distributes the heat more evenly. As the oven goes through its preheating cycle, make your other necessary preparations. Put your mold or molds in place on the forming table, and put a sheet of plastic into the frame.

Lower the frame containing the plastic, letting it rest directly over the oven.

Test the readiness of the plastic by quickly tapping the corners of the sheet with your finger. The corners always heat more slowly than the center. When the corners are soft and pliable, the plastic is ready to use.

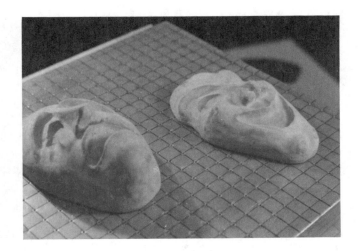

The forming table is perforated with a pattern of small holes, one in each square inch of its surface. The holes are connected by means of a valve and some associated plumbing to the vacuum holding tank.

Transfer the frame to the forming table, press down hard, and open the valve. The vacuum tank immediately will begin to fill with air from the room's atmosphere.

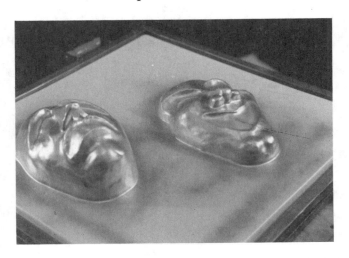

The opening in the flip-flop frame is just a little larger than the surface of the forming table. When the frame is forced down on the table, the soft plastic contacts the table edge on all sides and forms an airtight seal. Since air cannot leak in around these edges, this maximizes the pressure that the pattern on the table receives from the atmosphere.

As the tank fills with air, the vacuum pulls—or, more accurately, allows the atmosphere to push—the plastic down tightly against the pattern.

After the plastic sheet cools, it will retain its new shape. The formed pieces can now be cut from the sheet of plastic on the forming table and removed.

Now that you have a general idea of the vacuum forming process, let us examine, in the next section, the steps in the construction of the vacuum forming machine.

MAKING A VACUUM FORMING MACHINE

A vacuum forming machine for theatrical use can be constructed in a variety of sizes. Our 4′ × 4′ table, mentioned earlier, is large enough to make textured coverings for scenic walls. A shop might wish to build a 2′ × 8′ table to be used specifically for vacuum forming columns and cornice mouldings. The machine demonstrated on the following pages works with a sheet of thermoplastic two feet square; this is a good size for forming property items.

Although the construction is not difficult, it would be unreasonable to expect that a novice will sit down with these instructions and single-handedly turn out a machine by following them. Some special tools and specialized knowledge are required. We are confident, however, that any high school theater organization could build this machine with the cooperation of the metal shop, electric shop, and wood shop teachers. The wood shop could provide the basic chassis and the forming table; the metal shop, with their special tools and skills, could make the clamping frame and oven housing. Someone with electrical experience is needed to install the various control circuits to keep the unit safe and in compliance with local electrical codes.

If you like the idea of building a machine with a 2′ × 2′ format, then all of the engineering has been done for you; just follow the specifications given here. If for some reason you decide to alter the dimensions (there is certainly nothing sacred about the 2′ × 2′ size), someone on your staff must make the necessary modifications to the basic scheme. For some suggestions on implementing design changes, refer to the section on Making Modifications (page 190).

We chose the 2′ × 2′ size for the following reasons:

- *Economy of material.* We can readily obtain 4′ × 8′ sheets of plastic from West Coast distributors. A sheet this size can be divided into eight 2′ × 2′ pieces, leaving no waste.
- *Intended use.* The table is a good size to construct most theater properties.
- *Storage.* The machine is convenient to store when it is not in use. The finished size is 2′3″ × 4′8″.
- *Cost.* The construction of a machine this size is relatively simple and the expense is in keeping with its usefulness.

The Clamping Frame

All the measurements for all the parts of any vacuum forming machine are calculated from the dimensions of the flip-flop clamping frame. The size of this frame should be determined chiefly on a basis of its intended use and on economical usage of the available plastic sheet.

Make a frame of ¾″ square metal tubing. Weld the corners. The frame shown is square, and its outside dimensions are exactly 24″ on each side.

Hinge the two halves of the frame so the frame can securely grasp the plastic sheet, sandwiching it between the two parts of the frame.

Study the photo at left for suggested placement of two essentials: grips and thumbnuts.

Glue #50 carbide grit to the inside of the frame with a high-temperature rubber cement or epoxy cement. (It has been our experience that the temperature of the frame never exceeds 180°F.)

When you tighten the wing nuts, the frame clamps shut, and the grit bites into the edges of the plastic, holding it in place.

If it is used for an extended period of time, the frame may become uncomfortably warm. Wooden handles fitted to the frame permit you to continue working even if the frame gets hot.

There is a 5″ extension designed into the lower end of one of the frames. The frame pivots (or flip-flops) on this extension. It is fastened to the chassis with two pairs of brackets, one on each side of the bed. Use two ¼″ bolts (secured with hex nuts) for hinge pins.

The Oven

The oven heats the plastic sheet to its softening point (about 300°F.). The distribution of heat must be uniform. If a small area of the plastic receives too much heat, the plastic stretches thin, becomes transparent, and finally forms a hole. If the corners do not get enough heat, they remain rigid, preventing an effective air seal along the edges of the table. In the presence of such a vacuum leak, the casting will surely fail.

Your heat source could be gas, electricity, or even a bank of infrared lamps. We will demonstrate construction of an electric oven. Heating with electricity is safer and allows greater control of the heat distribution across the oven floor.

The top of the oven measures 24″ in each direction (the outside dimensions of the clamping frame). It has a ¾″ rim around the entire top edge to protect the clamping frame from direct

contact with the heat source and to direct the heat to the plastic sheet where it is needed. The depth of the oven chamber is 5″; the walls taper 1½″ on each side, making the oven 3″ wider in both directions at its base. The tapering walls are important for reasons explained below. We will also take advantage of the extra room at the base to add another heating element.

Make the floor of the oven from a rigid insulation material. It must be resistant to both the transmission of heat and the conduction of electric current. The floor of the oven in the photo is a panel of calcium silicate ⅜″ thick, which can tolerate temperatures up to 500°F. Later, when we build the side walls, we will use the same material to insulate and protect the side walls from overheating.

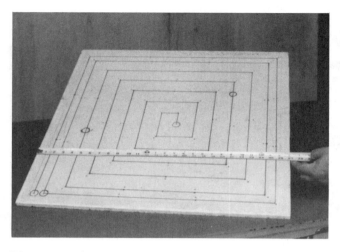

Fit a metal or masonry blade in your saber saw and cut the insulation board to size. It should be a square, 2′3″ on a side.

With a marking pen, lay out a spiraling maze design on the insulating board. Put 2″ between each line of the maze. This design represents the placement of the heating coils.

Make a mockup of the oven walls with ⅛″ Masonite. Join the four walls temporarily with masking tape. Save the mockup; you will use it later as a pattern when you cut out the oven walls.

Heating Element Design Considerations

The center of the plastic sheet in a vacuum form receives almost twice as much radiant heat from the heating coils as it does around the edges. The heating elements may be distributed absolutely evenly across the floor of the oven, and still the distribution of heat is surprisingly un-

even. There is a tendency for the center of the plastic sheet to get hot, the perimeter to be cooler, and the corners to remain cold.

The tapering walls give us an additional 3″ of space around the base of the oven. Use this room to accommodate one more heating coil around

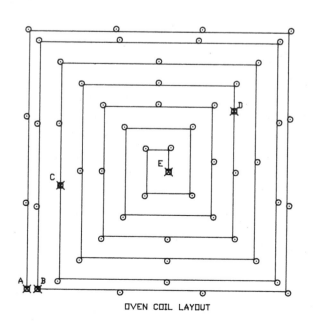

OVEN COIL LAYOUT

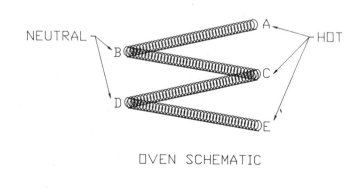

OVEN SCHEMATIC

the perimeter of the oven floor. Place it closer to the next outermost coil than the rest of the coils are spaced. Make it 1″ from its neighbor in order to intensify the heat around the outside edge.

The oven heats the plastic sheet in two ways, both very effective:

• *Radiant heat.* Preheat the covered oven for twenty minutes before forming the first sheet of plastic. Direct heat radiates from the coils of wire

and from the heated oven bed. The extra outer row of coils increases the amount of radiant energy available from the heating elements to the edges of the plastic.

• *Convective heat.* Heat is transferred to the plastic from hot air movement inside the oven. The 1½″ slant of the side walls helps to direct air currents, concentrating them toward the outside edges of the frame.

Making the Heating Elements

Our 2′ × 2′ oven requires a heating element 382″ long. We will convert this long element into four segments, each 95½″ long. Physically severing the wire is not necessary. The wire can be divided into four segments by inserting electrical taps in three places. You can identify the taps as heavy-lined points on the lefthand drawing on page 182, labeled A, B, C, D, and E.

The schematic diagram at the lower right on page 182 may help you visualize this concept.

The two drawings on that page are electrical equivalents.

Correctly wired, the four coils are parallel, each drawing 115 V. When we finish winding the heating elements (as outlined on this page and the next), we will have four parallel circuits; each will draw 5.2 A at 115 V and have a power rating of 600 W. The *total* oven wattage (four circuits) is 2400 W, drawing 20.8 A.

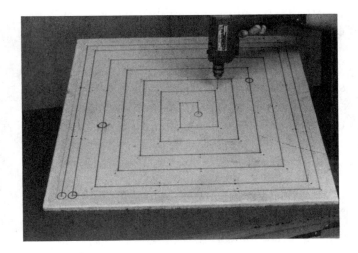

Drill a ³⁄₁₆″ hole at each point where the heating coil will turn a corner. Drill additional holes spaced every six to eight inches along the wire's route. Drill holes for the terminal posts B, C, and D. The terminal posts fall directly in line with the coils; the rest of the posts are to be offset, falling alongside the coil's path.

Mount a ceramic post on a ³⁄₁₆″ × 1½″ machine screw at each of the holes, securing the screw with a nut on the underside of the board. Mount an additional tapping post at points B, C, and D. These posts will be wired with wiring lugs under the table.

Winding the Coils

Obtain 88′ of #22 nichrome wire to make the heating coils. This is enough wire to make four circuits, each exactly 22′ long.

Stretch the wire out in a straight line and accurately measure the four 22′ segments. Flag the measurements with short pieces of tape; then

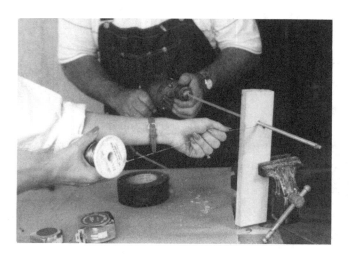

Have your assistant apply gentle tension to the wire, feeding it carefully alongside the piece of wood. The increased diameter of the rod (by virtue of the windings) will automatically feed the rod slowly through the block of wood. The windings are remarkably tight and neat. As you progress, the flags marking the 22′ segments will wind onto the rod. We chose to cut the wire at the 44′ mark (the midpoint) in order to make

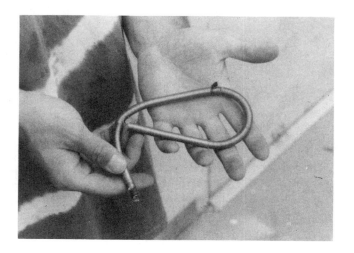

re-roll the wire back onto the spool to make it easier to handle as you wind the heating coils.

You will need a winding jig to make the coils. To make the jig, you need a variable-speed electric drill, a 2′ length of ¼″ rod, a piece of scrap lumber with a ¼″ hole, a vise, and an assistant.

Secure one end of the wire to the ¼″ rod. We did this by drilling a small hole in the rod and threading the wire through the hole; you might be just as successful securing it with masking tape. Attach the end of the rod nearest to where the wire is secured to your electric drill.

There does not need to be great tension on the wire as it is wound. Turn the drill motor slowly as shown, and the wire will coil easily onto the rod.

the coils more manageable.

When you finish the coil and release the tension, the windings will spring back just enough to allow you to slide the coils smoothly off the rod.

The process of winding the coils is really very simple. Once the winding jig is assembled, you should be able to finish this step in the construction process in as little as ten minutes.

This little coil of wire will make up two of the oven's circuits. The piece of black tape identifies the center of this piece—the point at which it will be attached to post D. First, though, we must stretch the coil to a length of 95½″.

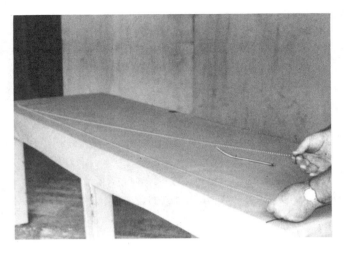

Loop the flagged point on a nail, grasp the free ends of the coiled wire, and walk away for a distance of 95½". The wire will be a little springy, and it is likely to fall short of 95½" when the tension is released. Pull it harder, till it stays the proper length even when it is not under tension.

Stretch the other pair of wire coils in the same manner.

Fasten the flagged center point of one length of wire to terminal post *D*, and one free end to terminal post *E*. Distribute the windings around the maze pattern, keeping the tension equal along each segment of the path. Attach the coils to the ceramic with short pieces of soft wire. Attach the other free end of the long coil to ter-

minal *C*. Space the remaining coils evenly between the posts, and attach them with short pieces of wire. The oven is now one-half wired. Finish wiring the oven with the remaining segments of coils. The midpoint this time attaches to post *B*, and the free ends connect to *A* and *C*.

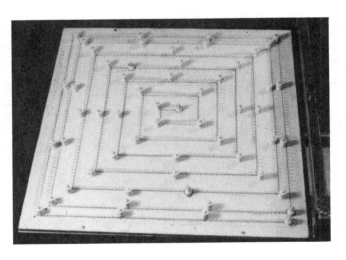

This oven is now completely wired. The four wire segments, each 95½" long, have been distributed between posts *A* and *B*, *B* and *C*, *C* and *D*, *D* and *E*.

It might be interesting to point out that the outermost square of this maze (from post *A* to post *B*) contains exactly one quarter of the total heat energy of this oven.

Building the Chassis

The chassis of the vacuum forming machine supports the oven, the forming table, and the clamping frame. The space under the forming table accommodates the vacuum pump, the vacuum tank, and the control circuits (switches, valves, and wiring).

The framework measures 2'3" wide and 4'8" long. The lower portion of the split level supports the oven and is square — 2'3" in each direction. Its upper rim is 5" lower than the top of the table side, to allow for the height of the oven walls.

We chose to construct this frame of square metal tubing, but a wooden framework of 2 x 4 fir would serve just as well. We put the frame on casters; you may decide these are unnecessary.

The same calcium silicate composition millboard used for the oven floor should be cut to protect the sides of the oven from becoming excessively

Using the Masonite mockup as a pattern, construct the oven walls. The oven must be made of a non-flammable material. We used flat mild steel: 1/8" x 4" for the angled side walls, 1/8" x 1/2" for the rim around the top, and 1" angle iron for the base. All seams were welded. If it is more convenient for you, you could make the walls of 18-gauge sheet metal, overlapped and riveted at the seams.

hot. Cut the pieces to size and fasten them inside of the metal walls.

The clamping frame should lay perfectly flat on top of the oven walls. When it is flipped over to the forming table it should lie squarely on the platform.

We are now ready to tackle the construction of the forming table, the vacuum pump, and the related plumbing.

The Vacuum System

There are several components in the vacuum train. The worktable "bread board" in the photo at right shows how the plumbing is hooked up. The parts are connected just as they will be when they take up residence inside the framework of the chassis.

1. Vacuum pump (and motor)
2. Check valve
3. Air filter
4. Vacuum tank
5. Pressure sensitive switch
6. Vacuum gauge
7. Valve (electrically controlled or manual)
8. Forming platform

The vacuum pump evacuates the air from the tank. When the vacuum reaches about 25 in / Hg the pressure sensitive switch is actuated and the pump is turned off. The check valve automatically closes to keep the air from flowing back into the tank. If there are no leaks, the vacuum will hold and the system is in "stand-by mode," ready and waiting to form a sheet of plastic. When the sheet is in place, the valve is opened and there is a rush of air through the perforations in the forming table as the atmosphere fills the tank. That rush of air will pull the softened plastic with it, forcing it firmly against your pattern.

Let us examine each of these components in detail, beginning with the forming platform. This is the one part you must make for yourself; the rest of the components can be purchased or scrounged.

The Forming Platform

The vacuum system terminates in a platform on the forming table. This little platform is actually an air chamber that evenly distributes the effects of the vacuum over its entire surface.

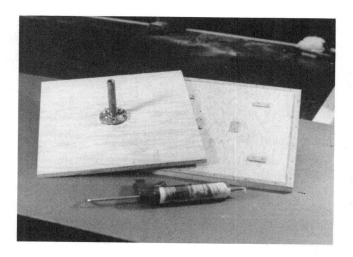

Make the forming table by sandwiching ¼" plywood strips between two square panels of ¾" plywood. The machine we are making requires that the large plywood squares be cut to 21½" on a side. (Remember, the forming platform must fit inside the clamping frame.) Apply an unbroken border of strips around the perimeter, and dot the interior with a pattern of spacers as shown. Use silicone caulking to seal the spacers as you nail them in place.

Cover the top piece of the sandwich with sheet metal. Wrap the sheet around the edges of the plywood, making the corner edges smooth and slightly rounded. The heated plastic sheet that will be formed on this table must make an airtight seal when it contacts this smooth edge.

Lay out a grid of lines 1" apart over the entire surface of the forming platform. Drill a hole ⅛" in diameter at each intersection.

Cut a 2" hole at the exact center of the bottom side of the lower sheet of the sandwich. Attach a floor flange threaded to accept ¾" water pipe. Use the caulking liberally to ensure that this connection is airtight. Nail or screw the two halves of the platform sandwich together, and the forming table is finished.

Vacuum Pump and Vacuum Tank

The pump should be capable of evacuating the air from the tank in approximately two minutes.

A thirty-gallon hot water tank has a volumetric capacity of about four cubic feet. A vacuum pump rated at 10 cfm (cubic feet per minute) will easily evacuate the air from this tank in two minutes. "Gast" vacuum pump model #1065 is one such pump.

Check Valve and Air Filter

Place a check valve and an air filter in the line between the pump and the tank. The air filter is necessary to keep rust and other contaminants from being pulled from the tank into the rotating fins of the pump. It is likely that an air filter will come with the pump when you buy it. If not, the retailer who sells you the pump should be able to sell you a filter.

The check valve is a device that allows air to pass through in one direction only. It automatically closes when the pump is turned off, preventing a reversal of the air flow. Otherwise, the atmospheric pressure would force air through the pump and back into the tank, dragging the pump and its motor in a backward spin.

Pressure Switch and Vacuum Gauge

The pressure switch senses the amount of vacuum in the tank and turns off the motor so it doesn't run continuously. The pressure switch operates at any pressure or lack of it. The actuating pressure is controlled by turning an adjusting screw. You could eliminate this part by keeping your eye on the gauge and throwing a toggle switch manually each time you want to control the motor.

You will need a vacuum gauge to set the pressure switch and to occasionally verify the machine's operation. You will not need to look at it often, however, unless you choose to operate the motor manually.

Valve

We installed an electrically operated valve. Our clamping frame makes contact with a microswitch as it is forced over the forming platform. This switch opens the valve, and the effects of the vacuum on the hot plastic are immediately apparent.

Here again, you may choose manual operation, and install a stopcock. It is just as effective, if not quite as convenient.

Making Modifications

The biggest challenge you will encounter if you attempt to make a larger vacuum forming machine will be in designing an oven that heats evenly over a greater area. The problem of cold corners is intensified. A large sheet of plastic sags as it softens; the closer the center gets to the heating element, the hotter it becomes. You may be forced to form the sheet (to avoid burning a hole in the center) before the corners are ready. Here are some ways to compensate if the corners and edges remain too cold:

• Use an oven cover, and preheat the oven to encourage convection heat. We use such a cover on both of our machines, although it does tend to slow the efficiency of our operation.

• Wind the outermost heating element with a heavier gauge nichrome wire. This will increase the heat around the perimeter, but it will also increase the amount of power needed to operate the oven.

• Use the same gauge wire, but space the outer coils closer together. This also increases the oven wattage.

• Be selective about how the coils are spaced; use closer spacing for the first six inches or so nearest the corner, "normal" spacing along the straight run, then closer spacing again as you approach and turn the corner, etc.

Designing the Vacuum System

The following design suggestions use ballpark figures, but these figures provide a useful starting point for planning the tank and pump needed for any size vacuum forming machine.

• A 48″ square table is four times as large as a 24″ square table, not twice as large. All of the plumbing must be planned taking into account four times the air flow. Where the 24″ table used ½″ plumbing, the pump, valves, and associated pipe fittings should be 1″ for a 48″ table.

• The tank should have about one cubic foot of capacity for each square foot of area on the forming table. A 48″ forming table has an area of sixteen square feet, so there should be about sixteen cubic feet of air space in the tank. A 120 gallon tank would work fine for this size forming table. (Each cubic foot is roughly equal to 7.5 gallons.)

• Vacuum pumps are rated according to their ability to move *unrestricted* air. A pump's efficiency decreases in proportion to the increase in vacuum pressure. In other words, the initial movement of air from the tank is rather fast, and the final phase of evacuation is comparatively slower.

• A vacuum pump rated for 20 cfm (cubic feet per minute) will evacuate the tank in a little over two minutes. Our 48″ table uses a Gast pump, model #2565, rated at 20 cfm, requiring a 1½ hp motor to power it.

A larger vacuum tank is more difficult to obtain as a found item. The tank must have thicker walls to withstand the air pressure of the larger surface. This makes it very heavy—and costly. If you cannot find a sixteen cubic foot tank, you may be forced to buy it. You may even have to order it specially constructed in order for it to fit in the space under your table.

Safety Considerations

As styrene heats and softens, it releases some fumes, but these are not toxic. There are also odors generated, and some people find that long exposure to these vapors causes slight eye irritation and watering. These fumes are heavier than air and collect in the lower portion of a closed space. Provide good general ventilation to mini-mize this irritation.

If through negligence you allow the styrene to heat past the softening point and into the melting and smoking stage, the fumes from the smoke do become dangerous. Under these circumstances you are exposed to the dual danger of fire and toxic fumes.

Most thermoplastics begin to soften at temperatures between 220°F. and 300°F. Therefore, the oven portion of the vacuum form gets hot enough to be a safety consideration. The danger is greater than that encountered with a domestic baking oven, because this one has an open face. Be careful not to allow yourself or anything else to fall into the oven.

Once removed from the heat source, the heated plastic poses no threat to safety because it loses its heat within seconds of making contact with the forming platform and the pattern. I have never known the hot plastic to be a source of danger to the operator.

Our oven includes a grid of ½" hardware cloth installed directly over the heating coils. The grid protects the operator from accidental contact with the heating coils which could result in burns or electrical shock.

Another dangerous feature of vacuum forming which must not be taken lightly is encountered when one begins to cut and trim the plastic with a mat knife. Our crew has experienced a number of cuts, nicks, and scrapes as a mat knife slips on the tough plastic and flies uncontrolled into the softer yielding flesh of the hand holding the plastic sheet. These cuts can be very serious. The admonition to "cut away from yourself" is an excellent rule when you are trimming plastic.

SUMMARY: Ventilate the work space for comfort, removing stagnant air and offensive fumes. Exercise great care to not allow the plastic to heat into the smoking stage, releasing toxic smoke. Use care with the oven (as you would with any heater) to avoid burns. Cut away from yourself (and others) as you trim the plastic.

MAKING VACUUM-FORMED CASTINGS

The Pattern

The vacuum forming process requires a positive mold. The casting will be a thin-shelled reproduction—also positive. The pattern must be smooth and firm, able to withstand the force of one atmosphere of pressure, and able to resist the momentary heat received from the sheet of plastic.

Solid objects of wood, metal, ceramic, or plaster make excellent patterns. Many authentic objects produce successful vacuum formed reproductions. Patterns made of thinner materials, such as unsupported Masonite or sheet metal, could easily collapse under the pressures of forming, but even these can be used when reinforced with internal bracing.

Sculptures made of Plasticine clay or rigid urethane foam cannot stand the momentary high temperature involved in vacuum forming. The heated plastic melts the surface of the pattern, making a release difficult—but not, as we will see, impossible.

On the following pages we will examine all of these materials and demonstrate ways of using them successfully as vacuum forming molds.

Using a Hard Pattern as a Mold

Objects made of wood and plaster usually make ideal vacuum forming patterns. The sides should slope gently from the forming table to the center of the mold; the pattern should contain minimal undercuts and have no deep depressions on its face. Such a solid object can be used with no further preparation than simply setting it on the forming table.

It is not unusual, however, for a pattern to have deep recesses in its surface which trap air and thus cannot be fully acted upon by the vacuum. Such a pattern requires a little extra attention.

The lack of detail around the eyes and mouths of these castings results from an air seal which has formed around the ridges of the eye sockets and lips. The only way to achieve finer resolution in these areas is to provide a channel which allows air movement out of these recesses. These cavities must feel the vacuum's full effect until the plastic is smoothly hugging their inner walls.

Filing an additional wrinkle in the corner of the eye is one way to obtain the needed air path.

Drilling a hole that goes all the way through the mold to the surface of the forming table is the more direct method of providing this airway.

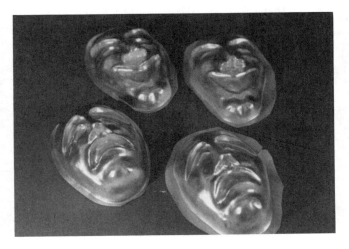

In either case breaking the air seal results in finer detail, as is evident in the second pair of castings, on the left.

When you can use an authentic item as a vacuum forming mold, the thin plastic castings will be very realistic.

This mold is a pattern of real roofing tiles, caulked with plaster.

Reinforcing Thin-Walled Patterns

If you have chosen a pattern with thin walls to use as a mold, it is possible that the pressures of vacuum forming will warp or crush it. Filling such a fragile pattern adds the strength it needs.

A common filling agent is wet clay. Any form of clay, however, placed in direct contact with the forming table, will tend to clog the small suction holes. Protect the holes from this kind of contamination by laying a piece of loose weave cloth between the pattern and the table.

The cavity of a thin-shelled mold can be filled with Plasticine when only a few reproductions are required. Repeated castings, however, eventually transfer so much heat to the clay that it softens and loses its effectiveness as a reinforcement. Even this problem can be overcome if you have a refrigerator nearby. Control the temperature of the mold by occasionally placing it in the freezer unit for a few minutes between castings.

A fragile shell might also be filled with wet plaster. When this has set, the form will be as strong as if it were made entirely of solid plaster.

One final filling material can be used to add strength quickly to a pattern of thin cross-section.

Clay and Urethane Sculptures

When you do not have an authentic object to use as a mold, your first impulse may be to sculpt a suitable pattern from modeling clay or rigid urethane foam. Unfortunately, these two modeling materials are both subject to a surface melt on contact with a plastic sheet that has been heated to 300°F. Separating the bond is impossible without destroying either the mold or the casting. That's the problem, and, curiously, it is also the key to the solution.

You can form a releasing surface on urethane

Rigid two-part polyurethane foam can be mixed and poured into the cavity. (This product is discussed in detail in the section on Two-Part Urethane Foam [page 149].) When the foam cures, the thin-shelled mold will certainly be firm enough to withstand the rigors of vacuum forming.

foam or clay molds by vacuum forming a skin of polystyrene directly over the original sculpture, *melting it into the mold, and leaving it there.* Vacuum formed polystyrene will not adhere to polystyrene. So the plastic jacket functions as a mold release for all future castings. This skin should be as thin and form fitting as possible. Use 20 mil or even 10 mil styrene if you have it in stock. Be aware that a thinner plastic sheet heats to flow state much more quickly than a 30 mil sheet.

The pattern for this family crest is 3' × 2'6", and it nearly fills our larger forming table. We assembled the crest using a variety of materials. The central shield and the small flag standards are wood; the lion, unicorn, helmet, and crown are carved from urethane foam; and the lower trim (leaves, ribbon, and rosettes) are sculpted Plasticine.

The vacuum formed sheet of styrene unifies the texture of the various materials, and in a real sense welds the individual elements together. If we had needed only one coat of arms, this casting could have been trimmed, painted, and mounted as is. It would be a little heavy but certainly usable. However, we needed four copies; so we trimmed this pattern, made no effort to separate the pieces, and laid the whole unit on our forming table. Using it as a mold, we made four additional castings.

Compare the similarity of this mold, sculpted of urethane foam and covered with polystyrene as a releasing skin, with the mold reinforcing tech-nique described on page 193— a polystyrene shell filled with two-part rigid urethane foam as a stiffener.

You can also apply a jacket of styrene to a rough-textured mold if you experience difficulty in separating it from your castings.

A plaster mold imitating flagstone or brick be-comes crumbly when it is repeatedly pried from its castings. This is not a matter of surface ad-herence, but because of constant friction created by the slight undercuts.

A styrene shell formed over any coarse, un-even texture assures that you will get an easy release from the mold without losing the rugged character of the pattern.

Other Mold Releases

A parting agent is not necessary on most surfaces other than Plasticine and urethane foam. If the thermoplastic sheet does not melt into the mold surface, it is usually self-releasing. Sometimes release from a found object can become difficult if the object is coated with paint. The heat of repeated castings transfers to the painted surface, and the paint becomes tacky. An application of silicone spray puts a slick finish on the pattern and ensures the desired easy release.

Producing Multiple Patterns

The designer supplied us with a single wooden baluster which he had turned on a lathe.

He wanted us to make twenty-four full round copies for use in the construction of this balustrade. (The production is *A Yard of Sun*, and the designer is Ed Wright.)

We bisected his wooden rail support on a band saw to produce two identical halves. These wooden patterns could be copied on the vacuum form twenty-four times to produce the required number of castings, but this procedure would waste a lot of material. We wanted a plan to make

We decided to make a vacuum formed copy of the wooden halves, and using these two plaster shells as molds, fill them with plaster. By using this casting process three times, we finally had eight patterns (two wood and six plaster), enough

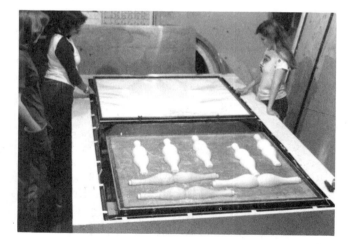

more efficient use of our large forming table.

Obviously a few more "originals" would be helpful. As was noted earlier, plaster molds work fine on a vacuum forming table. So we thought about ways we could make several plaster forms from the two existing wood patterns.

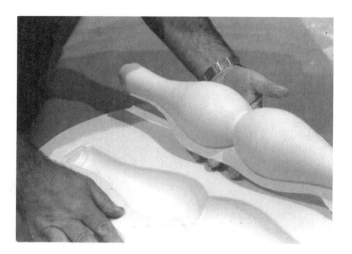

to completely fill our four-foot forming table.

We produced plaster copies of the wooden originals at the rate of one pair every half hour. Working steadily, we had six plaster molds ready in about an hour and a half.

Loading the eight molds onto the table, we formed our first sheet of styrene, and we were soon ready to trim the castings and cement the eight halves together.

Cutting and Trimming

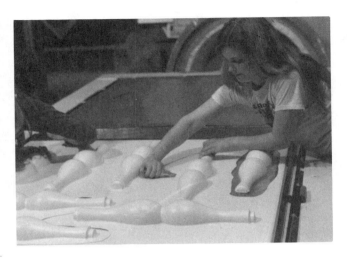

As you cut the individual castings from the plastic sheet, take care to never forcibly press the tip of the knife into the surface of the table. This would scar the table and dull the blade of your knife. Draw the blade through the plastic with the knife almost on its side.

The table surface may still be marred, but the scoring should not be excessive.

Once more, be warned to cut away from your body. A slip with the knife is not unusual; when it happens, make sure the blade is not directed at yourself or a friend.

Trimming the excess plastic from the casting can sometimes be a very time-consuming project. On a complex casting the trim lines seem to go on for miles.

You can cut 30 mil polystyrene with scissors, a mat knife, or an electric knife.

Electric Knife

An electric knife uses electricity to heat the tip of the blade. The hot blade reduces the plastic to liquid, and the thin cutting edge slides easily through the resultant puddle. The drawback to using an electric knife is that the slightest pause in cutting heats the plastic past its melting point and into the burning stage, producing smoke — *and that smoke is toxic!*

Scissors

Scissors are useful only when the border of the casting is straight enough to allow the scissor blades access to the cut. Curves and contours often make use of scissors impractical.

Mat Knife

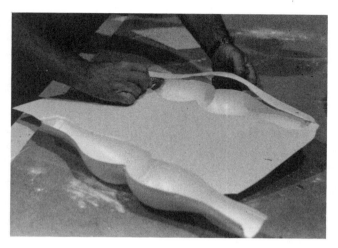

Very thick castings (60–80 mil) can sometimes be cut on a band saw, if the trim line is straight and uncomplicated.

A mat knife is usually the best tool for trimming vacuum formed plastic. As you trim excess plastic from the formed shape, hold your mat knife on its side, keeping the sharp blade parallel to the flat surface of the scrap. The blade slides along, using the flat surface as a guide. Once this technique is mastered, you can make perfect, effortless cuts far superior to those made with a pair of scissors.

Making Splices

There are several ways of making splices in styrene. The pieces can be joined with hot glue, fastened with masking tape, or welded.

Welding Plastic Joints

Nearly-perfect splices—ones that will stand up to very close inspection—are made using styrene cement. This cement (really a plastic solvent) melts the surface of each piece of plastic. Pressed together and allowed to dry, the pieces become welded. The solvent is variously labeled "styrene cement," "acrylic cement," and "thermoplastic cement." All solvents are not universally effective on all thermoplastics, but the acrylic cement you may be familiar with as a Plexiglas solvent is readily available and works well for styrene.

We will continue with the balustrade project to demonstrate how to make a splice with styrene cement.

Reassemble the two halves of the wooden pattern by nailing them together. Fitting the plastic pieces around the original form guarantees perfect alignment as you weld the first seam. Place two of the plastic shells around this form so that their edges overlap about ¼″.

Use a small, inexpensive (or expendable) brush to apply the cement. Dissolved styrene will get into the bristles, and although it is possible to clean the brush in the solvent, it is a reasonable certainty that the brush will have a short life. The photo shows an acid brush in use.

Dip the brush into the solvent and apply it between the halves of the casting where the edges overlap. The dissolved surfaces will bond together. The solvent dries very quickly, so the weld will hold in a minute or so and can attain maximum strength in as little as fifteen minutes. Use a small piece of masking tape to hold the seam together while it cures.

When you have a series of castings to join as we did in the baluster project, the work can go quickly because you don't have to be inactive during the drying periods. You can go from one piece to another, gluing one, taping it, setting it aside to dry, gluing another, taping it, and so on.

When the first welded seam has cured, remove the wooden form from the casting. This will submit the seam to a fair amount of pressure, but the shell's flexibility should keep the seam from rupturing during this maneuver.

Repeat these steps to cement the opposite side of the baluster.

So far the seam has been made strong, but it may not stand up to close inspection. Repeatedly painting the joint with solvent blends the sides of the seam together and makes the splice smoother.

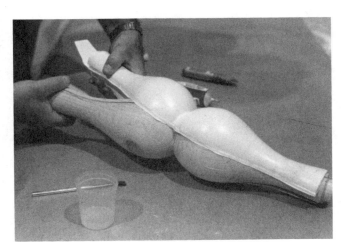

There is another cement on the market, rightly called "thick cement," which can help make the join invisible. It contains a transparent filler and will bridge across gaps and mismatches. The manufacturer recommends thick cement for use in making the initial weld, but it dries more slowly than the plastic solvent and, in my opinion, is better suited to blending, filling, and hiding the joint *after* it has been welded.

Unless the use of the vacuum formed item dictates it, there is usually no profit in spending the amount of time that this kind of seam treatment requires. Most splices on scenic pieces can be made by bridging the gaps where the pieces join with masking tape.

Masking Tape

As a student I was taught that no responsible theater technician would be caught using masking tape for any purpose other than that for which it is marketed—controlling the overspray on a unit being prepared for painting. I still hang on to this doctrine, but I now make one exception: that of repairing flaws that form in the seams of styrene panels. In fact, with the wisdom of my years, there is a temptation to believe that masking tape *really* was designed for the sole purpose of sealing joints in vacuum formed styrene. It works that well.

Use 2" masking tape for most splices. If you apply it smoothly, you don't have to be shy about the amount of tape you use. Press the tape down to make a close fit, and burnish it with your fingernail, forcing it to cling tightly to the clean plastic.

In applying tape to irregular surfaces, give lots of freedom to the fit. Don't pull the tape tight—give it all the fullness it needs to fit into the contours. We have found that you must use crepe-backed masking tape for this operation. Smooth-backed tape lacks the necessary elasticity. Use the stretch and flexibility provided by the crepe to get into the hard-to-reach portions of an irregular surface.

The value of vacuum formed plastic as a property or scenic element would be sharply reduced if we were deprived of the use of masking tape!

Hot Glue

Certain formulations of hot glue are very useful in joining polystyrene. Hysol's Formula 1946 is especially good. The heat transferred by the hot glue is sufficient to melt the styrene momentarily, producing a very strong heat bond. The seam may be a little bit rough, but when it is coated with a cosmetic covering of masking tape, the seam becomes smooth and quite presentable.

Oversized Castings

Vacuum formed plastic sheets do a good job of masquerading as mouldings, cornices, or decorative wood panels. There are several good reasons for encouraging the use of plastic to pull off this deception:

1. Sheets of .030″ (30 mil) polystyrene are cheaper than ¾″ plywood by as much as two thirds.

2. Formed plastic mouldings and cornices are about 75% lighter than the equivalent item made of wood.

3. There is a saving of about 50% in fabrication time.

These figures are true, however, only when you construct the mouldings in quantity.

Look out for the trap! If you only need 12″ or even 15″ of finished moulding to decorate a set you are building, it would be a mistake to acquire it through the vacuum forming process. You would be wiser to build the pattern and apply it directly to the set, using it as the finished piece of moulding.

Be assured that we *did* need a large quantity of wood paneling for a production of *Travesties.*

The motif repeated continuously around the room with some minor variation.

It was decided that vacuum formed copies of a very few simple patterns could produce this décor and would be economical in terms of both materials and labor. We grooved and tooled twelve feet of 1 × 12 pine to make the mold. In the procedure described in the following paragraphs, we cut the 12′ length of pine approximately into thirds, filling the forming table and making efficient use of the plastic sheet.

Vacuum forming tables are typically designed to copy relatively small-area castings. Our four-foot machine, which is large for a private shop, is still rather small when one is talking about making mouldings. The clamping frame that grasps the plastic takes up a couple of inches, so the longest run of moulding we can make is 3′8″. This means that we must make a splice every 3′8″ along any linear run of vacuum formed moulding. In working with long runs of cornice mouldings and panel strips, splices become a way of life—but they're not difficult.

(It is true that commercial machines have been built for movie studios and major special effects shops that will handle 4′ × 8′ and even 4′ × 12′ sheets of plastic, but they are a completely different matter.)

A Plan for Making Splices in Styrene Moulding

When you need a long, straight run of moulding, plan from the beginning for a means of making the joints.

Flat surfaces of thin sheet plastic are susceptible to buckling. Any time you can find an excuse to design an angle, rib, or low relief pattern into the mold, you profit by having a stronger casting. The bullet nose bead that is a part of this moulding design has added greatly to its solidity.

Nail a ¾" strip of pine to the end of the pattern before you begin to shape and tool it. As you rout the pattern, the shape from the main body of the pattern will be continued onto this nailing strip.

When you have finished shaping the pattern, pry this strip off and then nail it back in place — but attach it so there is a slight offset, like a

stairstep, in the pattern's surface. Make this off-set in one end of each section of the pattern that you construct.

Drill a few small holes in places that you suspect might become sealed and not draw air properly.

(This problem was discussed in "Using a Hard Pattern as a Mold," pages 146–147.)

These holes work as a continuation of the network of holes in the forming table, and therefore become part of the vacuum system, ensuring that the vacuum affects those hard-to-reach sections. An ⅛" hole drilled in the deepest part of the grooves will not show up in the finished casting.

As you form the styrene sheets, the slight offset will appear in each casting. This tier allows each successive run of plastic moulding to nest into its neighbor, producing a nearly invisible joint. The surface of the joint becomes almost flush and avoids creating a shadow line broadcasting its presence.

Two splices in the horizontal runs of this moulding can be discerned. But the vertical runs have also been spliced, and their seams have disappeared completely.

Framing Oversized Castings

Roof Tile

You met this roof tile during the discussion of Using a Hard Pattern as a Mold (page 193). Now we will take up the subject of making a frame and joining the vacuum formed castings into a larger unit.

While the prop room was producing multiple copies of the roof tile pattern, the scene shop was busy constructing a wooden frame to support them.

A full-scale floor plan was drawn on the shop floor, and the roof supports were constructed directly on top of this layout. The exact size and shape of the roof and all of the correct angles were built into the support frames.

Arranging the plastic sheets side by side and stapling them to the frame is a relatively uncomplicated task.

When you apply vacuum formed sections of large, heavily textured panels such as these roof tiles on a frame, don't expect them to fit perfectly. Holes, gaps, and mismatches are sure to

appear. The mismatches should not be a matter of great concern.

Just fill these imperfections with criss-crossed applications of wide masking tape. Don't be miserly with the tape; use whatever is required to cover the gaps at every joint.

The last coating of tape must be applied smoothly, without any of the telltale wrinkles associated with masking tape. Burnish down the edges of the tape with your fingertips or fingernails, to be certain that the tape has made good contact everywhere with the plastic. Once paint is allowed to get under the edges the tape will never lie flat, and the raised edge glaringly calls attention to itself.

When the unit is painted, the masking tape will accept the color in exactly the same way as the plastic sheet. All joints completely disappear. You can expect to see the evidence of this successful blending as soon as the base coat is applied. Later, when the tiles have been textured with highlight and shadow tones and have received a contrasting spatter, the seams simply cannot be found.

The finished roof unit should be the first piece of scenery to move onto the stage. It should be flown up while the wall flats are assembled under it, and then the frame can settle down onto its nest for the run of the show.

Cornice Moulding

Theaters without a vacuum forming machine at their disposal frequently reject the notion of cornice mouldings because these large mouldings are difficult, expensive, and time consuming. Vacuum formed cornice moulding goes together much more easily, cheaply, and faster than similar mouldings made of other materials.

Vacuum formed cornices don't come for free, though. A 10″ × 5″ moulding, and the associated framing to keep it straight and secure, could be built in 1989 for about eighty cents a foot. In proposing this budget, it is assumed that you will get about seven feet of moulding from a single four-foot square piece of polystyrene, and that you will keep the pine framing simple.

Another trap that one may fall into is the temptation to make the framing too complex. Don't do it! The vacuum formed styrene should contain all of the form and decoration; the framing should do nothing more than support the lightweight styrene shell.

Producing cornice mouldings is one of the things your vacuum form does best.

Construct your mold so it has a slight inset on one end, similar to the one described in A Plan for Making Splices in Styrene Moulding (pages 202 and 203). This difference in levels will again aid in making invisible splices.

We have had opportunities to use this same vacuum form pattern for making both a plain and a more ornate moulding. The strip of decoration that is being added here is itself a product of vacuum forming. Its low relief is strong, and it can become a working member of the mold without being reinforced.

These frames have been cut to fit the walls of a set. A stack of trimmed vacuum formed cornice moulding is ready to be applied. All that remains to be done is for the pieces to be spliced together, the angles cut on the ends of each piece, and the runs mounted at the top of the walls. Simple? Well, at least not overwhelmingly difficult.

Attach the vacuum formed plastic moulding to the wooden framework with staples.

Splice the plastic with a hot glue gun. Make sure you select a glue stick recommended for use on polystyrene.

When the splice has been made physically strong, make it cosmetically beautiful with repeated applications of strips of wide masking tape.

Once you have the angle plotted with an angle divider, you can miter the ends of the cornice with a band saw so they fit at the corners.

Try to make this angled cut on an un-spliced short piece of the plastic before splicing it into the long run of cornice. It is certainly easier to handle shorter pieces on a band saw.

If the walls of the set can be assembled on a wagon and rolled onto the stage as a unit, you can attach the cornice to the walls and make the corner splices before the moulding is painted. If not, you will have to paint the cornice in the shop, and then attach it and tape the corner joins onstage—and do a lot of touch-up painting.

Prepainting the Plastic Sheet

You can paint and texture clean polystyrene castings with the same water-based acrylic paint that you use to paint scenery. The dimensional aspects of vacuum formed plastic are enhanced by using standard painting techniques. Brick, stonework, roof tile, and stucco can be simulated with an application of the appropriate color; then the necessary aging, shadowing, and distressing can be done with either a brush or spray gun.

A problem can arise, however, when you try to apply carefully controlled fine lines on a dimensional vacuum formed piece. The facets and high relief interfere with your brushwork if you attempt to paint wood grain, marble, or stencil patterns.

The answer to the problem is this: do the intricate painting on the sheet while it is still flat, *before* it is vacuum formed.

Painting the Sheet

Keep the paint mixture as thin as possible. In heating the plastic sheet you will be approaching the heat tolerance of most paints. Thick coatings of paint are more prone to scorching and are liable to form white hairline cracks where the

Paint the styrene sheet in any pattern the design calls for, no matter how complex.

Work with the sheet flat, and keep the coatings thin. Dyes, inks, and metallic powders have especially interesting effects on white styrene.

plastic stretches around the pattern. It is the practice of some shops to form the sheet of plastic while it is still wet with fresh paint, in order to combat the hairline problem.

Vacuum Forming the Painted Sheet

Load the plastic into the frame so the painted side faces the direct heat of the oven. Your operators must be sensitive to the fact that overheating will discolor the painted surface. Form the piece as soon as the corners of the styrene become soft.

If you find that even with great care you can't prevent the direct heat from scorching the paint job, here is a method you might try: Un-bolt the

gripping frame from its bracket, and lay it over the oven, keeping the painted side of the plastic away from the heat source. When the sheet has been heated sufficiently, lift it off the oven; without flipping it over, transfer it to the forming table and press it down onto the forming platform—with the painted side of the plastic still on top.

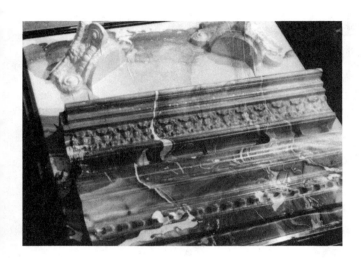

When you decide to prepaint the styrene, you must be prepared to accept the fact that there is not much you can do with it after it is vacuum formed. You may attach it to a reinforcing framework with hot glue or staples without marring the finish, but splices are almost out of the question. A small amount of touch-up might be possible, but it will be difficult.

A FEW PROJECTS THAT DEMONSTRATE VACUUM FORMING TECHNIQUES

Making a Marble Clock

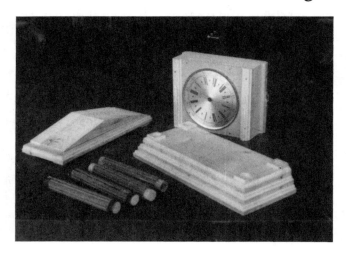

Cut the clock body, its base, and its pediment from pine. The pillars are ⅝″ dowel covered with corrugated cardboard. (One surface of the cardboard has been removed to expose the ridges.)

The face of the clock in the photo was salvaged from a real clock that was no longer operative. However, a clock face can be easily cut from sheet aluminum and dressed with decal or rub-on Roman numerals.

Distribute the pieces on the forming table, allowing enough space between them so that webs do not form. (This photo and the next show the vacuum form being used to make several similar projects simultaneously.)

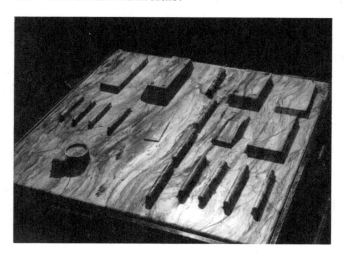

The vacuum formed sheet of prepainted styrene hugs the wooden parts, going almost all the way around the pillars. Trim the plastic, but make no attempt to remove it from the pattern. The painted plastic shell will remain with the wooden form for the life of the prop.

Cut the styrene away from the tops and bottoms of the pillars and the sockets where the pillars fit into the base and the pediment. Secure the pillars with white glue, and the clock is finished. It will withstand close inspection, and no touch-up painting should be necessary.

Vacuum Formed Books

A *very* lightweight shelf of books can be assembled from vacuum formed castings.

Make the pattern by cutting up some old discarded books on a band saw. Remove most of the book, leaving only about an inch of the body attached to the spine. Hot glue the book backs to a strip of ¼″ plywood to keep the unit manageable. (This strip could actually be put into service as a row of lightweight books, dressing the shelf of a setting. But let's say, for the sake of pursuing this demonstration, that the set needs more books than we have available spines.)

Spread the book backs out on the forming table in what you consider to be a desirable arrangement. The photo shows how three sections could be grouped — one long row and two shorter ones. The smaller leaning sections will be used on the ends of a shelf. Don't forget to keep the lower edges of the books lined up, even though some books may be at an angle.

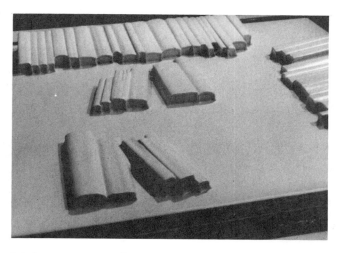

Make a vacuum formed copy of the carefully laid out patterns.

Free the rows of books from the sheet of formed polystyrene. Pry the book backs from the shell and trim the excess plastic.

Make a wooden frame with Masonite ends to stiffen and support the vacuum formed shell. The Masonite ends are made to look like book covers.

Be careful not to use *too much* bracing in this support, or you will defeat your original purpose. Remember, wood has weight.

Use masking tape to join the shell to the Masonite covers and to make any repairs that may be necessary.

Paint the "bindings" of the plastic shells with book-like colors. Use a small brush to sketch in some fake titles.

Here is the vacuum formed shelf as it appeared in a production of *Travesties*. The real books at the center of the lower shelf were needed for a piece of stage business.

Vacuum Formed Leaves

Within a period of six months, UCLA produced two plays that were each set in a jungle. The first of these was produced in the winter of 1983. This was a Guatemalan play called *Soluna*. The designer, Rich Rose, asked for two banana trees to help dress his jungle set. Six months later he designed Tennessee Williams' *The Night of the Iguana,* which is set in a tropical forest.

If you do a thing often enough, you get good at it. We got pretty good at making banana trees.

Preparing the Mold

Mature banana leaves run from seven to twelve feet long. We have to put these leaves in the "oversized" category, since we certainly could not make one-piece castings on our 3'8" forming table. There will have to be at least two splices in the leaf, maybe three.

We made two plaster castings from real banana leaves to serve as the vacuum form molds. We doctored one mold so that it could be used to form both the stem end and the leaf tip; the other formed the leaf's mid-section.

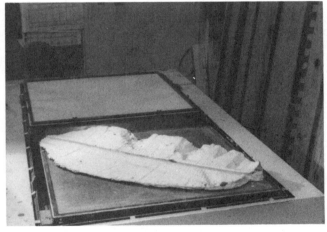

The leaf used as a pattern to make the first plaster mold must be altered somewhat with a pair of scissors. First it must be shortened to fit the table. Then the truncated end must be clipped to resemble the original leaf tip, so this leaf fragment has the appearance of an intact leaf. The vacuum formed copy made from this mold will be cut in half and an extension spliced into the middle. When this leaf and its center extension are assembled, the three-part casting will be about eight feet long.

This mold is made from the middle section of a long leaf. It must also be trimmed so it will fit on the vacuum forming table.

Forming the Leaf

Vacuum form several copies of each pattern, and trim the surplus plastic from the edges with a pair of scissors.

Making the Splice

Banana leaves are usually wind-torn in many places. Take advantage of this fact when you join the sections together. Make a splice at a place that could be a natural tear line. Take care to stagger the tear lines, or the leaf may become excessively weak at these joints.

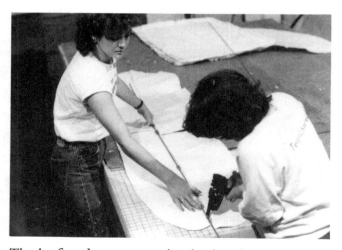

Glue an aluminum tube up the middle of the stem to reinforce the splices and give the leaf strength. Without this ''spine'' the leaf would collapse under the pressure of its own weight. A wad of hot glue every foot or so is sufficient to hold this tube in place.

The leaf under construction in the photos above is about seven feet long. The diameter of the metal tube is about ¼". Leaves ten or eleven feet long need a ½" tube to give them the needed support.

Run a strip of 2" masking tape up the center of the leaf to keep the tubing in place. The tape also blends the tube into the shape of the leaf and keeps it from looking like a hardware add-on.

Paint both sides of the leaf with at least three coats of acrylic scene paint. The base coat will blend the masking tape and the styrene and make them one texture. (It always does.) The second coat should be a wet-blended leaf-like combination of yellows, greens, and blue. The third application should be a glaze coat of clear vinyl. These coatings will add a lot of body to the 30 mil polystrene.

Assembling the Banana Tree

You will find you can improve the appearance of the leaves by cutting more wind tears into them. These extra slits also allow the leaf to follow a more natural curved line.

Force a droop into the width of the leaf by bending it hard along its spine. The leaf, reinforced with the 2" masking tape and the heavy paint job, will stand up very well under this pressure.

Form the treetop by shoving the aluminum stem of each leaf into one of an array of larger tube receptacles built into the top of the trunk. Then bend the aluminum stem into a curl that has a banana-leaf "look" to it.

We were fortunate in the scenic design for our production of *Soluna*—the banana trees peeked out over an eight-foot wall. The trunk was completely hidden, so all we had to build was the treetop.

A Vacuum Formed Marketplace Display

Lay a tray of artificial fruit (or five pounds of real fruit) on the forming table, and make a vacuum formed copy of it. Trim the casting, glue it to a plywood disk, paint it—and it becomes a permanent prop that cannot bruise or rot.

The display at left shows (clockwise from bottom left) a tray of peaches, a basket of oranges, two lugs of table grapes, and an unpainted tray of apples—all vacuum formed copies.

Making a Lightweight Statue

Reproduce any statue or bust in a lightweight form by casting it in vacuum formed polystyrene.

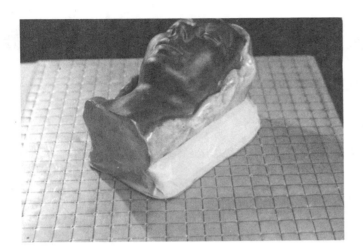

Make a bed of Plasticine on the underside of the pattern. Without this protective bed, it would be possible for the concave plastic under the model to pull thin or even develop a hole.

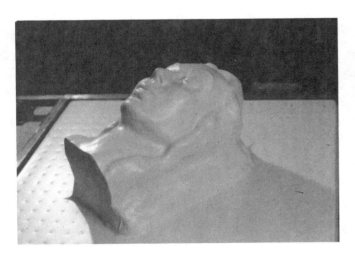

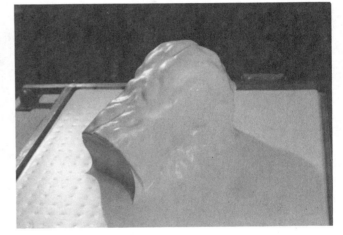

Make two vacuum formed copies of the pattern: one of the front and one of the back. In each case, support the model on a bed of Plasticine and leave more than half of the model exposed.

Glue the trimmed castings together to make a complete three-dimensional copy. You can plan where to make the join, hiding the seam by having it coincide with a prominent feature of the pattern. The splice on the head in the photo runs along the concave ridge of hair near to the hairline.

Making a Lightweight Headdress

A great variety of hats, masks, and headdresses can be made entirely or in part using vacuum forming techniques. The pair of antlers shown below is representative of this group in at least one sense — it is lightweight.

Select an authentic set of antlers to use as a pattern. Make castings of the front and back of the antlers (the same technique that was used on the last page to vacuum form the statuary bust). After the halves have been trimmed, join them together with glue.

Vacuum Forming Transparent Plastics

Acetate, acrylics (including Plexiglas), and a product of the Eastman Kodak Company called ''Uvex'' are all transparent and formable in a vacuum press.

The vacuum forming process can be used to make complex-looking stained glass panels with raised features, expensive-looking door and window inlays, and custom designed shades and globes for lighting fixtures.

Transparent plastics begin to fog and lose their transparency if they are allowed to heat to their melting point. It is important that you form a transparent plastic just as it softens, and before it begins to melt.

This casting was made from ⅛″ Uvex, using wood carvings as the patterns, on our two-foot forming table.

Making a Sphere

In the past, the accepted technique for making a large globe or other spherical object was to cover a weather balloon with a hard shell of papier-mâché or Celastic. Now with a vacuum forming machine you can make a globe from two perfectly shaped hemispheres, and you can do it with ease.

Your sphere or dome could even be transparent!

The ''form'' for a hemisphere is nothing more than a large plywood box, open on the bottom, with a large perfect circle cut into the top. The depth of the box must be somewhat more than the radius of the circle.

Allowing the open end of the box to rest on the forming table, seal the box to the table with masking tape and use the tape to seal all the joints of the box. The box becomes one large vacuum chamber, extending the force of the vacuum to the circular hole cut into the top of the box.

Remove the clamping frame from its pivot bracket. After the plastic has been heated as usual, lift the frame from the oven and rest it on top of the box. The plastic makes contact with the plywood face with the circular hole, and as the vacuum is applied, a perfect hemisphere is formed by the plastic being drawn into the interior of the box.

You must exercise very careful control with the valve to draw the sphere deep enough to make a sphere, without pulling it too deep. It might be necessary to make a couple of imperfect castings to learn just how to manage the valve.

Excessive stretching of the soft polystyrene makes the plastic extremely thin at the deepest point of the concavity. Thirty-mil styrene becomes like tissue. We used 80 mil for our project, and the globe was still very fragile at both poles. Delicate areas such as these can be strengthened by filling them with two-part urethane foam.

When you have two perfectly formed hemispheres, trim away the excess plastic.

Cut a disk of ¾" plywood with a diameter the same as the inside diameter of the two polystyrene hemispheres. Drill a ½" hole through the exact center of the disk to accept an axis rod. Staple the two domes to the wooden disk around the "equator."

This standing globe was built for a production of Luigi Pirandello's *Right You Are if You Think You Are*. We made most of the woodwork by laminating double thicknesses of ¾" plywood together with PVA glue and air staples, making the wood 1½" thick. All of the raw edges of the plywood were routed to soften their appearance. The legs are stock table legs, obtained from a local lumberyard.

APPENDIX

Glossary

Absorption casting. A casting process involving a porous mold (usually plaster) and an appropriate liquid casting material. The mold draws solvent out of the casting fluid, causing the fluid to thicken where it contacts the surface of the mold. A thin wall is formed that conforms to the shape of the mold. When the wall reaches the desired thickness, the surplus casting material is poured from the mold. The casting hardens as it is allowed to air dry; then it can be removed from the mold.

Acetone. A solvent, very volatile, somewhat toxic, and highly flammable, used to dissolve paints, fats, and plastic resins.

Alginate. A mold-making material formulated from kelp. It has excellent reproductive properties and is non-toxic; it is widely used in making impressions for dentures.

Armorall. The trade name for a protective coating designed to seal vinyl and latex from the deteriorating effects of oxidation and sunlight.

Barrier cream. A protective hand cream which impedes the absorption of chemicals into the pores of the skin.

Bondo. A trade name of Dynatton / Bondo Corp. for a plastic body filler used in auto body and fender repair. (*see also* **plastic body filler**)

Cab-O-Sil. A thickening agent made of silica, used to fill and extend paints and resins. Syrupy polyester resin can be thickened to a paste with this product.

Casting (*noun*). A reproduction of an original pattern made from a mold.

Catalyst. A substance that precipitates, or increases the speed of, a chemical reaction. In the plastics of molding and casting, the catalyst affects the cure of thermosetting resins.

Celastic. A trade name for a casting material, formulated by filling a loose-weave fabric with cellulose nitrate.

Clay. A modeling material made of very fine particles of earth, softened by adding water, oil, or wax. (*see also* **Plasticine** *and* **slip**)

Clay sculpting tools. A set of implements specially designed to cut, chisel, trim, and otherwise shape modeling clay.

Dowman's Fixall. A trade name for a stucco-like patching material. This book suggests its use as a casting material.

Durham's Rock Hard Water Putty. A trade name for a wood putty. Castings with many of the characteristics of soft pine wood can be made from this product.

Dust mask. A protective face mask designed to filter fine particles of dust or mist and keep them from entering your nose and lungs.

EVA. *See* **ethylene vinyl acetate.**

Ethylene vinyl acetate (EVA). A thermoplastic material of the polyolefin family. In its molten state it adheres to many surfaces. This product is marketed commercially as a casting material and as a hot glue.

Exhaust fan. A ventilation system designed to remove toxic fumes from a working space and deposit them outside the building where they are diluted to an inoffensive level in the open air.

Freeze line. A flaw created when a thermoplastic casting material is allowed to cool unevenly during pouring.

Fume hood. A large inverted funnel connected to an exhaust fan. This environmental safety device is designed to capture and expel lighter-than-air toxic fumes from your work space.

Gloves. A protective covering for your hands. Gloves should always be worn when you are working with corrosive or dangerously hot materials.

Goggles. A protective covering for your eyes. Goggles should be worn when you are sanding or grinding, or working with chemicals corrosive to the eyes. Of special interest to those involved in molding and casting is protection from a splash of MEK peroxide, the necessary catalyst for polyester resins.

Hot melt materials. *See* **thermoplastics.**

Hydra-cal. A trade name for a mortar-like casting material, similar to plaster in its working characteristics but much harder when cured.

Impression coat. A carefully applied first coating of any molding or casting material. This coating prevents air bubbles and ensures universal contact with the pattern.

Keying notch. An alignment device for mating the members of a multi-part mold.

Kiln. An oven used for firing ceramic castings.

Laminated castings. Castings made by a process whereby thin strips of paper or fabric are bonded, with a glue or resin, in overlapping layers, against the inner surface of a mold.

Latex gloves. A covering for the hands, made of latex, designed to protect the skin from the harmful effects of the chemicals used in molding and casting. Two styles are popularly used. One type is available in supermarkets and is used for household cleaning and dishwashing. The thinner, disposable surgeon's glove is better suited to the needs of the mold maker.

Latex rubber. A liquid rubber that cures on exposure to the air to form a flexible skin. This material can be used for making both flexible molds and castings.

Liquid soap. A mold releasing agent. Tincture of green soap is sold commercially to be used as a mold release. Undiluted dishwashing detergent works acceptably also.

Material Safety Data Sheet. A publication required by law that every manufacturer of any material must make available to the consumer. This sheet lists the potential hazards of the product and proposes ways of using the product safely. You can obtain this sheet on any product you are interested in by writing to the manufacturer.

MEK. *See* **methyl ethyl ketone.**

MEK peroxide. A highly corrosive chemical used as a catalyst to cure polyester resins.

Methyl ethyl ketone. A solvent, very volatile, highly flammable, and toxic. Once recommended as a solvent for Celastic, it has been replaced, because of its toxicity, by acetone.

Model. A pattern from which a mold is made.

Mold. An object from which a casting is taken.

Mold release. A thin coating applied to the face of a mold to ensure that the casting will not adhere to the mold's surface but will separate easily.

Mother mold. A firm close-fitting cradle to support a flexible mold, forcing it to retain its true shape.

Moulage. A type of mold-making alginate which works in the hot melt process.

Moulding. A decorative strip or band of trim, made from wood or from plastic painted to imitate wood.

Negative form. A form (usually a casting made from a sculpture) that displays the features of a three dimensional object in reverse relief. A negative form of a face would show the nose and chin as deep hollows.

Neoprene. A synthetic rubber designed to replace latex. It is available in a liquid form which works in the absorption casting process.

Papier-mâché. A casting process involving a binder and one of several forms of pulp paper.

Pattern. A model from which a mold is made.

Petroleum jelly. An oil-based mold releasing agent, sold generically and under the trade name Vaseline.

Plaster (plaster of Paris). A material made of calcined gypsum, used in the making of both molds and castings.

Plastic body filler. A putty widely used in the repair of automobile bodies. It has a base of polyester resins and is thickened to a putty with sandable fillers.

Plasticine. A trade name of Peter Pan Playthings Ltd. for modeling clay; its plasticizer may be based in oil or wax.

Plastic Wood. A trade name for a wood putty. It has attained a reputation as a casting material among puppeteers.

Polyester resin. A syrup-like thermosetting plastic resin. It is available in a variety of formulations, useful in making coatings and solid castings, and as the bonding agent in fiberglass laminations.

Polyolefin. Any of a family of thermoplastics including polyethylene, polypropylene, and ethyl vinyl acetate (hot glue).

Polyurethane. *See* **urethane foam.**

Polyvinyl alcohol (PVA). A mold release which, when applied, forms a film of vinyl on the mold's surface. It can be applied with a brush, or thinned and sprayed. It is usually used in conjunction with a sealer and a paste wax.

Polyvinyl chloride (PVC). A family of thermoplastics including a hot-melt mold-making material and plastics used in upholstery fabrics and water and sewer pipes.

Positive form. A form that displays the features of a three-dimensional object in their original relationship. Objects such as your face, or a clay sculpture, are both positive forms.

Prosthetic alginate. An alginate specifically designed for making molds of body parts. This product differs from dental alginate in that it sets up much more slowly.

Prosthetics. A branch of surgery that specializes in providing amputees with artificial body parts. The meaning has expanded to include much of the three-dimensional work of theater makeup artists.

PVA. When referring to adhesives, these initials designate either a white glue made of polyvinyl acetate, or a glue (trade name: Elvanol) formulated from polyvinyl alcohol.

When referring to molding and casting this abbreviation stands for a totally different com-agent. *See* **polyvinyl alcohol.**

PVC. *See* **polyvinyl chloride.**

Releasing agent. *See* **mold release.**

Respirator. A face mask with interchangeable filter cartridges. It can effectively protect your nose and lungs from dust and mist particles or organic vapors by changing the filter.

RTV. Room temperature vulcanizing.

Silicone caulking. A flexible mold-making material which cures as the solvent evaporates in open air.

Silicone RTV rubber. A flexible mold-making material which cures when a catalyst is added to the silicone resin. Its vulcanization does not require external heat.

Slip. A diluted ceramic clay. It is used for making castings in the absorption casting process.

Slipcasting. A process of **absorption casting** using liquid potter's clay.

Sprue. An opening constructed in an enclosed mold which allows the casting material to be poured into the mold's interior.

Styrene cement. A solvent used to dissolve the exposed surface of a sheet of polystyrene. When two such wetted surfaces touch they melt together, making a bond.

Styrene sheets. A thermoplastic (polystyrene) in sheet form.

Thermoplastics. A broad classification of plastics which soften when exposed to heat, can be shaped, and will solidify, retaining the new shape when cooled.

Thermosets. A broad classification of plastic resins which cure to a solid form when exposed to a catalyzing agent.

Undercut. A bulge or depression in the side of a mold which precludes easy parting from a simple mold, and which therefore requires the construction of a multi-part mold.

Urethane foam. A commercially marketed foam product, available in either rigid or flexible form. The solid product is made for use as insulation; in its flexible form it is used in cushions and mattresses.

Urethane RTV. A two-part kit of urethane chemicals which can be mixed and cast into rubber objects with varying degrees of flexibility. Its vulcanization does not require external heat.

Urethane two-part casting foam. A two-part kit of urethane chemicals allowing the consumer to make custom-designed urethane foam castings.

Water extendable polyester. A formulation of polyester resin which allows the user to add water to the recipe as the resin is prepared for use.

Wax (paraffin). A mixture of hydrocarbons used in the manufacture of candles. Doll makers use this material to cast doll heads and limbs.

WEP. A trade name. *See* **water extendable polyester.**

Where to Get Your Supplies

Some of the products discussed in this book are so common that you should be able to find them anywhere.

Your local drug store or grocer will have:

Detergent (liquid soap)
Paraffin wax
Paste wax
Petroleum jelly

A large hardware store or paint supplier will have these:

Dowman's Fixall
Durham's Rock Hard Water Putty
Dust mask (particle mask)
Plaster of Paris
Plastic Wood
Silicone caulking

An automotive care store will stock these:

Armorall
Bondo plastic body filler
JB Weld (an epoxy-based
   metal repairing paste)

See "Artists Materials & Supplies," "Crafts Supplies," or "Hobby & Model Construction Supplies" in your telephone book Yellow Pages for these sculpting materials:

Clay
Clay sculpting tools
Latex casting rubber
Plaster of Paris

See "Candlemaking Supplies" in the Yellow Pages for:

Candle Wax

See "Welding Supplies" in the Yellow Pages for:

Leather gloves

Most of the materials of molding and casting can be found in a single retail store located in a large city, listed under the heading "Plastics—Raw Materials" in the Yellow Pages. In this store you should be able to purchase resins, their catalysts, fillers, mold releases, solvents, and protective equipment for safe use of the products.

Acetone
Barrier cream
Cab-O-Sil
Goggles
Latex casting rubber
Latex gloves
MEK peroxide
Methyl ethyl ketone
Plaster of Paris
Polyester resins
Polyvinyl alcohol
Respirators
Silicone RTV rubber
Styrene cement
Urethane RTV
Urethane two-part casting foam

Hastings Plastics
Santa Monica, California
(310) 829-3449

Plastic Mart
Santa Monica, California
(310) 451-1701

Other materials are more specialized and may only be purchased through the manufacturer or distributor.

We regularly use the services of several retailers in the Los Angeles area. The businesses listed on the following pages are eager to do mail order business if you have difficulty in obtaining the products locally. I suggest you call to verify price, availability, payment method, etc.

Alginate, dental alginate, prosthetic alginate.
Cinema FX
(A Division of—
Davis Dental Supply)
North Hollywood, California
(818) 765-4994

Celastic.
Alcone Co.
Long Island City, New York
(718) 361-8373

High impact styrene sheets.
Cadillac Plastics
(800) 521-4004
or

Plastic Sales Inc.
Los Angeles, California
(213) 728-8309

Latex rubber.
Chicago Latex
Crystal Lake, Illinois
(815) 459-9680
or

Cementex Latex Corp.
New York, New York
(800) 782-9056

Machinable wax.
Freeman Manufacturing & Supply Co.
Cleveland, Ohio
(216) 961-4200

Neoprene.
Chicago Latex
Crystal Lake, Illinois
(815) 459-9680
or

Cementex Latex Corp.
New York, New York
(800) 782-9056

Picco resins, Piccolastic, Piccotex.
Chemcentral
Santa Fe Springs, California
(310) 921-2100

Plaster (#1 pottery plaster, Industrial pottery plaster, Hydra-Cal)
United States Gypsum
(800) 621-9523

Water extendable polyester.
Ashland Chemical
Santa Fe Spring, California
(213) 946-3371

You will need products from some other specialized distributors is you decide to build a vacuum forming machine.

Abrasive grit
Trinity Tool
Los Angeles, California
(800) 881-4461
or

Metal dimensions
Los Angeles, California
(213) 582-1955

Millboard (calcium silicate panel); ⅜" Eterboard. See "Insulation Materials (Industrial)" in the Yellow Pages, or
Foundry Service and Supply
Torrance, California
(310) 328-1752

Nichrome wire (22 gauge). See "Wire" in the Yellow Pages, or
MWS—Magnetic Wire Specialty
West Lake Village, California
(818) 991-8553

Vacuum pumps.
Gast Vacuum Pumps
Benton Harbor, Michigan
(800) 952-4278
or

Brenner Fiedler
Cerritos, California
(310) 404-2721

The following pump accessories should be available from the same source that provided the vacuum pump:

Check valve
Solenoid valve
Vacuum gauge
Vacuum switch

. . . or from an industrial supplier such as:
Norton Sales
North Hollywood, California
(213) 877-0107
And if you decide to purchase a commercially made vacuum form, try these sources:
Z.M.D. American
Paramount, California
(213) 630-8826

or

Heartland Thermoforming
Great Bend, Kansas
(316) 792-2792

or

Orbit, Inc.
San Clemente, California
(714) 498-3001

INDEX